This issue is dedicated to the memory of photographer and humanitarian David Tacke, 1949 – 2017
Original Lost Lake Folk Opera masthead photo of the Lanesboro Dam
by David Tacke

Folk Opera

Fall-Winter 2017   Volume 4 Number 2

In This Issue

Nancy Lee sits down on the roof ledge facing the lake. I unfold a scarf to sit on. We each have an orange to peel. We stare out at the lake like old men sitting in rocking chairs on their porch, peeling oranges and rocking, deep in thought, and absentmindedly content. A ship is nearing the harbor but is still quite far off. Out above the lake in the watery blue sky, I picture my mother walking on her hands, a Chagall-like figure walking along a cloud, occasionally flipping upright to do the Charleston. Maybe Nancy Lee sees her mother dancing out there too, all dressed up, sophisticated and glamorous, instead of how she really is now, in a nursing home.

"Laos abuts the Mekong river as it idles by on its way to the South China Sea. Landlocked and slow paced in a saffron-colored Buddhist kind of way, the once named Elephant Kingdom seemed the perfect place for Don to rest his bones—the kind of place where time slows down and journey's end."

Lost Lake Folk Opera

Lost Lake Folk Opera is a Shipwreckt Books imprint
published twice annually.
Letters to the editor are always welcome.

309 W. Stevens Ave.	Rushford, Minnesota, 55971
507 458 8190	contact@shipwrecktbooks.com
Managing Editor	Tom Driscoll
Publisher	Beth Stanford

www.shipwrecktbooks.com

Cover art & interior graphics by Shipwreckt Books

SHIPWRECKT BOOKS PUBLISHING COMPANY L.L.C.

Rocket Science Press

Lost Lake Folk Art

Up On Big Rock Poetry Series

Lost Lake Folk Opera

WWW.SHIPWRECKTBOOKS.COM

Mr. Maryport
Lee Henschel Jr.

Excerpt from *The Sailing Master, Book Two: The Long Passage*

The eldest son of the Maharaja of Patna, Kota Singh, was always most eager for Mr. Botherall to play on his trumpet. But the recital usually took place in the middle of the night, long after the tropic heat had carried off, with Kota sitting in the palanquin atop his dhow. Certain the trumpet kept the off watch from their sleep. But it was a good thing, just the same, for Kota insisted Botherall play from the mizzen top, where each note would carry on the water. So as long as he played for Kota, then all of Three Madras would know the flagship's position, and stay closed up, at least until Percy's trumpet fell silent.

By Wednesday Island Three Madras had advanced well into the Pacific, making steady, if slow progress. Then Kota became 'sick of the sea,' as he called it, and convinced Admiral Wawne it would be a good thing to hole up in the nearest group of islands. Rendova. The Admiral agreed direct, for he'd already planned to take on fresh water in Rendova's leeward passage. There was also a deepwater bay where all of Three Madras might anchor. Only then, after Rendova, would the longest passage get underway. The Admiral wanted to be sure of our seaworthiness, for Cape Horn awaited.

The next morning, just at first light, Three Madras raised Rendova, and by noon line the Indiamen entered the bay. One by one they hauled their wind, and only after each ship swung to its anchor did *Tremendous* and *Eleanor* join them. *Spikenard* remained under sail, patrolling to seaward. Kota improved miraculous quick, and to mark the occasion he wished to invite the officers of Three Madras to dine with him on *Tremendous*, and listen to Mr. Botherall play on his trumpet. Captain Praerther placed my name on *Eleanor*'s list of attendees, not to partake though, but to serve as flag messenger for *Eleanor*. I didn't think much of that duty. I'd come to dislike the pomp of any flagship, and knew I'd be laughed at in Percy's old uniform, for it was still over large, and worn thin at the elbows. But certain I wanted to visit Percy. He was my best mate, and I missed his good nature. So I wore his old uniform during my watch on the quarterdeck, just to make sure it fit, at least in some places. When Praether saw me at the binnacle he frowned and called me aside.

"Ajax will be taking my gig to *Tremendous* when the forenoon watch is set. You will go with him. No doubt there's a tailor on board the flagship, so I'll write you a note instructing him to fit you out as a proper midshipman for Kota Singh's dinner. I'll have no representative of *Eleanor* dressed second-hand."

"Aye, sir. Sir, may I be permitted to ask a question?"

"What is it? "Will the tailor expect any payment, sir? Because I've no funds."

"The cost will be deducted from your pay ticket."

The deck officer came to address Praether.

"Beg pardon, sir, but the watch is set."

Praether thanked him, then turned to me. "Go."

I sat in the bow of *Eleanor*'s gig. Ajax stood tall in the stern, directing the two oarsmen to make for *Tremendous*. We made past the Indiamen riding at anchor, content as three cows in a pasture. The bay rose and fell, breathing most calm. The water ran turquoise under the gig, and broke gleaming white on the black-sand beach. A pair of kites soared in the light air, and the sky vaulted cloudless bright. Ajax pointed to the head of the bay, to the column of grey smoke rising from a village. A sidehill spring flowed there, and a dozen boats from Three Madras made for it.

We hooked on at *Tremendous*'s entry port, which opened on the middle gun deck. Ajax went off, leaving me to stand in a swarm of men going about their duties. I tried to gain someone's attention but no one paid heed, until a pimple faced midshipman stopped to look me up and down.

"Why do you stand there doing nothing?"

"I'm here to see the tailor."

"That would be Maryport. And if anyone's in need of a tailor, then surely it's you."

"See here, I'm a midshipman, same as you, and expect to be treated with the respect I've earned. So you will address me as Mr. Harriet, and direct me to Maryport."

My brisk manner took him aback, and he piped a different tune.

"Of course, Mr. Harriet. The tailor works in a small bay on the orlop, just aft of the powder magazine, port side." He pointed forward to a wide companionway. "That hatchway's the most direct, but mind you, the middle and lower decks are about to begin gun drill, and you must be sure to stand clear."

"Thank you. How will I identify him?"

"Maryport?" The midshipman laughed. "Oh, you'll know him. You just need to look low."

"How do you mean?"

"You'll see."

A gunnery officer screamed out a command. "Open ports."

"They're about to commence. You best make smart."

All along the deck every gunport yawned wide. The midday light poured bright through to reveal a fearsome line of artillery. Twenty-four-pound long guns, each piece crouching on its carriage. I counted forty-two of them. Twenty-one to port and twenty-one to starboard. Each gun stretched a full ten feet, and was served by twelve men and a powder boy. I kept well clear as the port battery stood to their guns, most eager to run them out. Soon the officer bellowed away.

"Port battery. Run out."

I'd heard *Eleanor*'s guns run out many times, and her rumble was a most terrible thunder, yet only a modest cough when compared to *Tremendous*'s frightful roar.

I wished to remain and observe the entire drill, but a midshipman must never tarry, so I gained the companionway and went on to the lower gun deck. Every gun port on the lower deck was shut tight, for they opened just three feet above the waterline. It made for a dark, overlong tunnel, with each gun lurking in shadow as a den of brooding beasts. But a lively den, nonetheless, for each section worked furious over its gun. The artillery on the lower deck was also ten feet long, but near twice as broad at the breech, for these guns fired thirty-two-pound shot. Soon the call came to open the gun ports. No doubt the guns would run out soon. Again, I wished to stay and watch, but instead made for the orlop.

The tailor's shop was in a small bay, not twenty feet long and but twelve deep, tucked between the bulkheads of the magazine and the sailmaker's shop. Bolts of duck cloth and wool dyed red or blue rest in narrow bins stacked to the beams. A work bench filled most of the bay, a cutting table twelve feet long, six wide, and raised three feet off the deck. A single lantern swung in its gimbal, shedding a dim light. Strange that, for no lantern on any ship is allowed to burn unattended, yet I saw no one.

"Is someone there?"

"Step forward and state your business."

The voice came full deep, and I thought it best to comply. Still, I saw no one, but then recalled what the midshipman had said. I must look low. So I did. And there stood a little man under the cutting table. I stooped to address him.

"Beg pardon, but I'm looking for Mr. Maryport. He's the tailor."

The man fixed me in his glare. "You're staring at him."

"Oh. I thought . . ."

"Thought what? That a person such as me is too nugatory to be a tailor?"

I didn't know the word nugatory, but Maryport's tone of voice gave it meaning clear enough. I thought to deny his accusation, but knew better, since it was true.

"You're correct, sir. I did think as much. I'll not apologize, though. Only try never to think you're nugatory ever again."

Maryport walked under the table, clearing it with ease, and came to stand before me. "At least you're honest. A dwarf rarely hears such a forthright reply. So I ask again, this time with more politick. What is it you want?"

I handed him Praether's note. "My Captain wishes you to make me a midshipman's dress uniform, for Kota Singh's dinner."

"That's tomorrow. I'm too busy."

"But Captain Praether says I must look the part of a proper midshipman and . . ."

"Praether, did you say?"

"Aye. Captain Praether. That's his note."

Maryport read the note and gave it back. "I've not heard of that once since Hull."

"Do you know Captain Praether?"

"Yes. But he doesn't know me. My sister's an acquaintance of Praether's wife, Cherish née Beverly. She lives in Hull. Our family's tailor shop is in Hull, and I sewed Cherish Beverly's wedding dress. That was five years ago, but I remember Praether well enough. He paid his bill on time and in full so I will honour his request." Maryport took out a scrap of foolscap and a pencil stub. "Come. I must take your measurements. I'm a hatter as well as a tailor, so we'll begin with a proper hat. Stoop! Hmm, you have very small head size. Stand tall now for the waistcoat. Breathe normal. No huff and puff. Frock coat next. Turn to your left. Now your other left."

"May I ask a question, sir?"

"What?"

"If you made his wife's wedding dress then certain the Captain must know you."

Maryport laughed scornful. "He would not. A groom has little interest in who makes his bride's gown. Now I'll measure your neck. Lift your chin. There, just so. And even if he would've taken an interest, still he'd not know me. Reach your arms out to the side. Oh . . . you're missing a finger. Did that hurt?"

"Yes."

"I'm very sorry. Now for your trousers. First your waist. You're a scrawny one. Take off your shoes. Stand flat of foot. I doubt you'll understand, but my sister would never mention my name to anyone outside the family."

"Because you're . . ."

"Yes, because I'm a dwarf. My family was always ashamed of me and they kept me hidden away, never to be seen or spoken of. So I ran."

"And the navy took you in?"

"They did. But just as a contract labourer. That's how it goes for one who doesn't fit in. Now your inseam. Your legs are very short. They barely reach the floor. But they'll make do."

"No, Mr. Maryport, that's not how it goes. Not always."

"What do you mean?"

"My brother Albert."

"He's a dwarf?"

"No. But he's simple. My Father and oldest brother are ashamed of him and keep him hidden. Same as you. But Mum and me, we love Albert most dear, and are proud for what he can do, if only you help him make a start of it. Except Mum's dead now, and I've been at sea over two years. I worry for him. He has no one to watch out for him. And he can't know how to run away."

Maryport cocked an eye, looking at me anew. "What's your name?"

I told him.

He nodded. "Kota Singh expects a new turban for his dinner gathering, but I'll make your dress uniform first."

"Thank you. It means much to me."

"More than Kota Singh's new turban will ever mean to him." He nodded at a bolt of white cloth rolled out on the table. "I'll cut his turban from that. It's a very fine weave, yet it means nothing to him."

"He must own a great many bolts of cotton."

Maryport laughed again. "Yes, a great many. And even more bales. He owns the entire consignment of Three Madras. The cotton's a bumper crop from Kot Kapura. Merseyside's sure to bid high. He's beyond wealthy. I pity him."

"Why?"

"Everyone laughs behind his back. The fool doesn't know he's to be held hostage once he reaches England. *We* all know it. But he does not."

"Then perhaps someone should tell him."

"No. The Admiral forbids it, and says it will go bad for anyone who tells Kota Singh the truth." He eyed me cautious. "But it seems you are one who values the truth, yes?"

"Yes."

"A worthy trait. Even so, it would be no lie of yours to withhold the truth from Kota Singh."

"I'm not certain of that, Mr. Maryport."

"Nor am I. But don't tell him, anyway."

He scratched a few numbers in a notebook, then tucked it away. "This will take several hours. I'll send it to *Eleanor* this evening. A collar as well, along with hose and leather shoes. Have you a dirk?"

I had no dirk, just a work knife. The Onion had taken my Arab blade when I became his prisoner.

"No, sir."

"I shall send one."

"The purser will take the cost of a uniform from my pay ticket, but can you tell me how much?"

"About three pounds. You'll pay nothing though because I won't submit a bill. Take the money and spend it on your brother. Go now. I'm busy." ◉

I know what's coming
4 poems by Andy Roberts

Grace

We caught a turtle
yesterday, the boys and I,
a painted turtle
big as a dinner plate.
Peed on Isaiah
when he picked him up,
scratched Earl on the pinkie.
Poked his head out
when we left him alone
in the cardboard box.
Ignored, with red unblinking eyes,
the lettuce and worms we left.
He wasn't much fun. The boys
forgot about him.

So this morning we
went up to Highbanks,
took the trail to Hayden Falls
with the turtle in the box.
Found a clear pool
six feet deep
below the falls
where the water slowed down.
Took him out of the box,
set him in the water
and let go.
His long neck stretched out
and all four legs
propelled him straight to the bottom.
Graceful and fast
in the clear water
where he lay on the bottom
and blended in.

We left after awhile.
But I'll keep
that image of grace
in mind
when I think
of the boys
that day
and the turtle.

Blues in February

All this talk about death
and I'm not even sixty.
Not yet. So and so
died last week
and how about
who sit and whatsit.
I don't want to hear it.
I know what's coming.
That's why you see me
at the window
staring at a bare branch
of the hackberry tree
on an early February morning.
Why I live in a house
with lots of windows.
Get up first,
pull the blinds open,
let whatever light forms
in.

Gadsden

Listening to Billie Holiday sing
Stars Fell on Alabama got me
thinking about the only person I knew
who moved to Alabama. Haskell Russell
moved to Gadsden to clean up a Burger King
daily from 3:00 am to 7:00.
He needed the work.

What I'm saying is there's a
combination of reasons why
we live the places we do.
My mother once dated a man
from Bird City, Kansas, who managed
to get out. I was born in Sault Ste. Marie,
Michigan, escaped to live all over
this country, and hope nothing
drives me back. It's so beautiful

the way Billie sings *We lived
our little drama. We kissed
in a field of white. And stars
fell on Alabama last night.*

Sold Jim
Joe Ducato

"Sold!" Jim felt the word. "Sold!' Sounded like it had been shouted from a mountain top, loud and bold as life itself, at least for the unafraid. "Sold!" Everyone called Jim "Sold". "Sold Jim." He'd been Sold Jim for as long as anyone could remember. If he's had a choice he would have picked a different name. Maybe *Big Jim the Auctioneer* or *Sir Large and Loud*, but Jim knew that man isn't the real creator of names. Nicknames are born of man's true nature. No, the one who lent him that holler was the same one who lent him the name—God. Well it's true God didn't actually give Jim the name but God did provide the rock to carve it in forever.

Auction-calling was never the only pear in Jim's basket. He had some other odd jobs under his belt as well. There'd been that summer gig at the Roadside Diner where Jim proved to be an amble clam-cracker and there was a short stint on the highway gang where he made center-line painting an art. Auction calling, though, that was the thing that really thickened-up Jim's stew.

At the Auction House, for many years, it was just Jim, Jim and the crooked-old-guy who owned the place. It was doubtful Jim knew ever knew his boss's name. The signature at the bottom of Jim's paycheck was an X. The crooked-old-guy barely talked and neither did Jim. After twenty years of working together they hardly knew a spec of information about each other.

The crooked-old-guy didn't trust anyone … not nobody. He kept the business' books under strict lock and key. Maybe that's where Jim got it from, all that distrust he had for people. Maybe he'd had it all along, and maybe it was just the crooked-old-guy that brought it out in him. Sometimes it takes someone else to stir our stew just the right way that brings for a certain flavor.

Jim and the crooked-old-guy were so much alike. It was a shame they never talked. They may have been good friends. They'd even developed moles on the same spot on their chins one time. That was a bit of a head scratcher.

One day the crooked-old-guy fell over and we nt belly-up on the hardwood floor and just like that, he was no more—simple as that. Nobody felt sad. Nobody shed a half of a tear for the crooked-old-guy but they did respect all the years he ran the Auction House.

Sold Jim kept right on working there even after crooked, old's son took the shop over. Jim referred to the kid as "Young Fancy Pants". The kid was different than his old man. The kid was straight and narrow for one. Young Fancy Pants could never bring it out in Jim like the crooked-old-guy could. That was a relief to Jim felt who his stew was thick enough.

One thing about old Sold Jim. He knew that fellow he looked at in the mirror every day. He knew him well, better than anyone else. He knew a couple things about himself. He knew he'd always need to work. Work was what kept his pencil sharp.

After the long-straight-kid drove the Auction House into the ground, Jim took on as a plumber's assistant. He never became "Let's Flush it Jim" or anything like. He was still Sold Jim. Liberace is still Liberace when he takes out the garbage. The smart ones know those laws. The other thing Jim knew about himself was that love was not for him. He knew that all day long. He'd seen what love had done to a couple of friends who couldn't defend themselves. No, Jim lived by two simple rules. You don't put your tongue on 210 volts and you don't swap souls with anyone but a Labrador Retriever. Love had its own rule, that being There ain't no rules. Sold Jim saw that people enjoyed love enough, it was just not his cut of meat nor Charlie Dead-Eye's for that matter. Charlie Dead-Eye was Jim's best friend. Charlie saw things straight like Jim even in his last days on Earth when the world got a little confusing to him.

Sold Jim was comfortable enough being the face in the crowd, although he did give his heart to a few things that couldn't bite him like the 2 Bs … big bands and billiards.

Sold Jim kept a steady course. Even after Deadeye was gone, Jim maintained a solid life— but in each no-hitter, there's that one pitch that got away, that one big mistake. Sometimes it doesn't come back and bite you, sometimes it just gets crushed. This is about Jim's one big mistake and what it did to him.

The seeds for the error were planted one Spring morning when Jim decided he'd do his walking at the fancy mall instead of the plain mall. You see the Auto Palace was at the fancy mall and The Auto Palace was having their big Spring wiper-blade sale and Jim needed blades bad. That proved to be the spark that would bring down the barn. Jim's bum knee also played a small role and soon you'll see why.

Jim arrived at the entrance to the Auto Palace that morning eager to save some bucks. To his chagrin there was a long, snaking line of customers who also badly needed to change their blades.

Standing in that line so long eventually weakened Jim's bum knee and soon he found himself leaning against this Turtle Wax display. Well, grace was never a tool in Jim's tool chest. It wasn't but five minutes before the heft of him sent the display flying, Jim flying and Turtle Wax cans rolling violently in every direction. One of the cans rolled straight into the leg of Ms. Gloria DeVane, who we will refer to, for simplicity's sake as *The Spider*. Ms. DeVane was adorned in faux fur and large hooped ear rings. She immediately turned to see where that wax can had come from and that's when she laid her eyes on the embarrassed Sold Jim. The widow DeVane was gifted with a lovely speaking voice. She almost brought it to Broadway once. Our boy never had a chance. *The Spider* went and helped Jim pick up all those cans and helped put the stand upright and by the time she and Jim reached the cash register, they'd made a real coffee date. What followed is in many ways the oldest story on Earth.

Jim and the widow DeVane met for coffee the next three mornings, and each morning he got a little reinforcing bite. Soon our boy was bringing little presents to Ms. DeVane, including a portable first-aid kit for the widow's car.

Jim was quickly lost to love. Turns out he was like all the rest of us after all, we who pray that we're bit at least once in our life-time.

Meanwhile, Charlie Dead-Eye was literally rolling in his grave. Jim the maintainer was suddenly tolerating things he never would have tolerated before, things like potpourri shops, flavored coffees, movies without violence and even diced-up fruit in a vegetable salad. There seemed to be no limits to the transformation. Jim couldn't even feel his bum knee anymore. That's how numb he was. Sold had a well-done meat flag stuck in his rump. All his buddies at McDonald's wondered where their reliable coffee buddy could have gone to and the tools on Jim's workbench cried like the orphans they were.

The dirty little secret is the world turns just one way. Those who know that know things that those who don't know that don't. Some folks get speechless when things begin to fly by them backwards. The folks who know things, know that a spider is always on the hunt for fresh blood. The folks who know things wouldn't have been surprised in the least to find out *The Spider* had spotted a new victim at Subway and that was that. She was gone in a flash to a new adventure.

Soon, Jim's phone no longer rang and his world filled with silence and not the good silence that feels like warm soup in your belly, but the other silence. The silence that feels like hunger. Jim got no "Dear Sold" letter, nothing, just hunger pangs. He hated himself more every day for going to that fancy mall.

The pure heart is a deep well. Folks with pure hearts know that their hearts can become anchors in the blink of an eye and the depths a pure heart can sink to are nearly incalculable. When the pure heart sinks, it's more than a sinking feeling. It can make folks do crazy things.

That's how it was with our boy. One day Jim took to walking. He just walked and walked, brooding about that anchor around his neck and then all of a sudden something snapped. The next thing he knew he had come to the conclusion that the only thing left to do was go climb a tree … and that's exactly what he did. He found a park and walked up to the most beautiful maple, one with, thick strong branches. He took two breaths then jumped up and grabbed hold of a branch. Well, it had been a long time and a large volume of jelly doughnuts since Jim had climbed. Oh, he gave it everything he had. He even leaked himself a little. It took six tries but on the seventh, he managed to heave his heft up onto that branch. He felt like he'd conquered the world. He sat up on that branch sucking in wind, then with trembling legs, stood and went for the next branch above. This branch proved easier to conquer. It was on! Jim lifted himself up to the next branch, then the next. The higher he climbed, the higher he wanted to go. If it wasn't for being so out of breath and his muscles being so flabby and his stomach being so big and his head feeling so light, he would have felt really great.

When he reached as far up in that tree as he could go, he let loose a rich and hearty "SOLD!" to the Heavens. He felt like he was Tarzan. He decided it was a great spot to set his sizable and scraped derriere. He made it his home. From his perch, he marveled at everything before him, marveled how it had all been designed by God. He was happy to find he had some "marvel" left in his soul.

It was all fairly beautiful until Mrs. Madeline Gleason, who lived in one of the houses bordering the park, stepped onto her porch to shake-out her dust mop, looked across the way and spotted this ugly, old bear high up in a tree. She went back in the house to get her binoculars. It was not a bear at all. It was our boy. She called 911 who promptly dispatched Patrolman Sims to the park. Patrolman Sims was new on the force, so new he pressed his uniform twice a day. Sims was proud of making the force. His mother saw him in a whole new way.

Sims slowly stepped out of his patrol car and cautiously went up to the tree. A couple of kids on lunch break from school were standing there too. Patrolman Sims warned them to keep their distance. He quickly taped off the area which was another way of shouting, "Hey everyone! Come look at this!" The widow Gleason watched intently from her porch. Sold Jim was amazed at how small Patrolman Sims looked from up there. Sims radioed in then placed a hand on his pistol.

"Hey," Sold Jim cried down, "I'm not dangerous."

"Is he a pervert?" one of the kids asked.

"Nuts sprouting early this year!" Mrs. Gleason whispered to no one.

Patrolman Sims tilted his head skyward.

"What is it you think you're doing up there?" Before Sold Jim could open his mouth, the answer came from Dead-Eye Charlie who was now standing next to Sims.

"I'll tell you what he's doing up there," Charlie said, loud enough for Jim to hear, "Love drove him up there. A broken heart drove that passion monkey straight up that tree if you can believe that!"

"Says who?" Sold Jim shouted down.

"Says me!" Dead-Eye volleyed back.

"What?!" Sims said spinning around.

"You ain't been right since that woman dug her claws in ya and you know it!" Charlie shouted.

"Yeah, and what right do you have to talk," Jim shot back fast, "You're dead!"

Sims looked annoyed.

"Who are you talking to?" Sims shouted up to Sold.

"A grown man hiding in a tree like a cat hiding from a dog. I've seen everything." Charlie Dead-Eye laughed.

"You're not supposed to be seeing anything!" Jim threw down.

Charlie Dead-Eye disappeared. The departed had departed.

Suddenly, sirens quickly filled the air and all heads turned to watch three fire trucks make their way into the park. They were clean and red and stunning. Moses couldn't have parted the seas with more grandeur. Three engines on one call. That hadn't been done since the Great Sears Fire of 1960. Everyone—the kids, the widow Gleason, Officer Sims, Jim—everyone was in awe. The arrival of the fire trucks even brought Charlie back.

The trucks all came to a halt and with their motors still running, nine firemen jumped off their rigs and started piling equipment onto their backs.

"Can we ring the bell?" one of the kids asked.

Patrolman Sims turned his attention back to the top of the tree.

"You're coming down one way or another!"

"I can climb down you numbskull!" Jim screamed in frustration.

"Not on my shift!" Sims retorted, "Get the bucket Curly!"
Fireman Curly tapped his friend, and together they started back to get the bucket ready.

It was precisely at that moment that an old man who was walking a small dog appeared. The old man had a pleasant face as did the dog.

"Just don't do anything to that tree," the old man pleaded.

Officer Sims looked at him curiously.

"This is where I proposed to my Maria. Right under that very tree. It was a day like today, very much like today."

"And you are?" Sims asked.

"Just old," was the man's reply.

Sold Jim yelled down, "You proposed to your wife under this tree?"

"Yes, I did," the old man answered looking up and using his hand as a sun visor.

"May the fifteenth. We go way back, this ol' tree an' me. We surely do."

"Your wife …" Jim started then stopped.

"Fifteen years," the old man said and looked away.

"I'm sorry," Jim lowered his eyes.

The old man tipped an imaginary hat and patted the head of his dog.

"Never hated anyone the way I hated that woman," the old man said, "I swear she was Satan's sister, but I miss the hell out of her. I really do."

The old man lowered his frame and sat on the grass then hoisted his dog up onto his lap.

"What's going on there?" the dispatcher's voice was heard over a fire truck's radio.

"Old guy and his pup," one of the fireman answered.

There was no mistaking the chopper when it came overhead. What a racket! What a sight. The pride of the news station. The widow Gleason yelled from the porch.

"WRPO says we got a jumper!"

A van belonging to the other news station pulled up to the scene as well. A team of folks jumped out and grabbed their cameras. The most stunning by far was Lindsay Willis, the six o'clock anchor. Lindsay was spotless and wrinkle free. She made Jim's heart skip and the old man's too.

Lindsay and her camera guy approached Sims.

"What's his story?" she asked.

"He ain't no damn jumper!" Charlie Dead-Eye muttered, "He don't even have the skills to fall out of that tree."

"Why is he jumping?" Lindsay asked Sims.

"Hey, you sound like you want him to jump" one of the kids said with indignation.

Patrolman Sims threw up his hands, "OK! Everybody! Get out of the way of that bucket!!"

Amid a cacophony of back-up beeps, one of the fire trucks slowly backed-up towards the tree. The kids sat next to the old man.

"Mind if we pet your dog?"

The old man smiled.

Somewhere out on the rich, green carpet, a lone figure was crossing the smooth land. The dark figure grew larger and larger as the stranger approached. The man, the figure, had something in his hand, something long and thin, a walking stick maybe. When he finally got to them, Officer Sims put up his hand.

"Stay away!" Sims warned.

Under the tree, the bucket was starting to go up. On the other side of the street, a small crowd had formed.

With one of the fireman in the bucket and another at the controls, the steady hum of the hydraulic lift dominated the air. Turns out the approaching stranger wasn't carrying a walking stick at all, but a metal detector.

"I said stay away!" Sims scolded a second time.

"Jump!" came taunts from teenagers across the road followed by laughter.

"Keep it rolling," Lindsay whispered to her camera guy.

The elderly guy with the metal detector ignored the officer's orders and faced Sims.

"I know your old man," he said getting even closer, "We were friends."

"I know you," Sims said staring long into the man's eyes, "You were the Police Chief, years ago, right?"

The man nodded then turned and smiled to the old man with the dog and the kids. Then he turned to the fireman, the one in the bucket and the one at the controls.

"You boys can put that thing down," the old Police Chief announced calmly, "I'm taking responsibility here. Go on now, lower that thing I said."

The man lifted the metal detector high so Jim could see it.

"Ever use one of these Mister?"

"No," Sold Jim answered.

"Best thing ever invented. Finds all kinds of valuables, all those little things people have thrown away or lost. You can have this one. I'll put it

against this tree. When you come down, try it. You'll be amazed."

The man propped the metal detector against the tree trunk then turned again to the old man and the dog.

"What do you say we wait for this good man to come down and then give him a taste of the good life?"

The old man nodded. The dog wagged his tail.

The old Police Chief turned to Sims.

"Go now kid. You did a good job. I got it … I mean we got it. Tell 'em it was me who sent you packing. Beautiful day. Not many like this, no sir, not many."

After everyone was gone and even Mrs. Gleason and her dust mop were back inside, Sold Jim came down from his tree of unrequited love. Charlie Dead-Eye had stuck around for kicks. He wished he could have chased love away for his old friend but he'd done a lot, especially for someone who was dead.

A couple of the new birds of Spring flew haphazardly overhead as the sun yawned on them. Somewhere in the park, three cats chased some squirrels. A couple of dogs barked at a couple cats, bees searched for love, old people walked and young people ran. The world turns just one way. Those who know it, know it. Those who don't, don't.

Later, when the sun had diminished to just a lullaby, they could all be seen walking, all dark figures. Looked like three men (one held a metal detector) a ghost and a happy dog. Turns out, it was a great day after-all. They carried treasure with them, a few quarters, a cross and just enough daylight to fit in a jar. ◉

www.shipwrecktbooks.com

Try to stay alive
Four poems by David L. James

Standing back up
for Dee and Derik

I'm off to another funeral,
this time, a young man,
a grandson of a friend.
I'm there, trying to be helpful
            and empathetic
but what can I do? Hold someone's hand?
Give a hug? Say I'm sorry for your loss?

I didn't know the kid, 32 years old,
the same age as my daughter. I can
imagine my heart being ripped out
of my chest if that was my cross
to bear. Nothing would be the same,
ever again. How do people stand back up
and walk across
the stage after so much pain?

Was it suicide? An overdose? Is someone to blame—
a woman, a boss, a friend?
I have no clue. But I kneel and pray
to God to spare me and mine from this flame,
though I know it's useless.

Dreaming of Spring
at the end of Fall

There's more to me
than skin
and bones, blood and hair.

I'm like this apple tree,
dropping fruit
with the slightest wind,
emptying myself
before winter arrives.

My leaves tear away, and I grin
like it doesn't matter, but it does.
I have to do this without help,
strip and dig my way
into another year of worry,
already dreaming of the day the snow melts
and I blossom again in your eyes.

Love/Birds

Lying in bed between his grandparents, Cloud (7) says,
"I'm floating between two lovebirds."

we're all floating/
drifting in & out of each
other's lives/touching hands & faces/
touching hearts & memories/
this one looks like a flower/this a peach/
here's a dark cloud/there's a broken vase

some of us flail & drown/
calling out beneath a blue sky/
but no one/answers/
some of us/before going down/
get lucky/find someone/tie
our fates together & float/
tossed around in the storm/
thanking the gods above

if you find yourself lying in bed/drifting like a boat
on love's water/you can be born
again/you can fall
asleep to the waves/the gentle lapping/
rocking back & forth/

/you may even believe/you have it all/

How I came to a revelation
in Michigan at the start of February

Another gray day
beats me silly with the promise

of nothing—
no sun, no light, no vitamin D,

no hope of climbing out of the abyss
of winter and walking into spring,

into love, into lying on the grass
where I would kiss your forehead

and talk of the years and laughter
to come. No, the forecast

calls for snow and ice to spread
across the state,

wind chill in the teens,
a darkness creeping under my skin,

up into my eyes, my certain fate.
Using pills or drink or caffeine,

I try to stay alive the best
I can. I huddle in the cave

of my house, bundle up for work, wander out
only to get more depressed.

Though I claim to be no slave
of anyone, I've been bought and sold,

chained and beaten by the world.
I stumble through each day like a blind man,

deaf to my heart's call, if the truth be told.

As a man
Two Essays by John Torgrimson

1. Golden Lilies

I noticed the delicate handmade slippers in a market in Beijing. No more than five inches in length, I held them up and looked at them from every conceivable angle before putting them back on the hawker's table.

When a Chinese friend asked if I knew what they were, I told him that they looked like baby shoes. "No," he said, smiling. "They're for the golden lilies."

When I looked perplexed, he said, "You know, bound feet."

I was stunned. "Surely no one has bound feet anymore?" I said, more as a statement than a question.

"Only very old women," he instructed. "Women who had their feet bound before Mao took over."

Foot binding was introduced in China as early as the eleventh century. At the age of three or four, a girl's toes would be bent down against the sole of her foot and fastened with tightly wound cloth. This painful process stunted the foot's growth and pushed the arch into an unnaturally sloped curve. The only part of the foot that remained in its normal state was the heel and the big toe, the rest of the foot rotted away.

The sight of a woman swaying back and forth on her pointed feet as she walked on her "golden lilies"—*like a tender young willow in a breeze*—was believed to have an erotic effect on men. And the smaller the lilies the greater the effect. Consequently, possessing three to four-inch delicacies would go a long way in advancing a woman's fortunes in seeking an eligible suitor.

But Golden Lilies prevented women from doing any manual work and for the most part kept them housebound, restricting their activities to the arts—embroidery and calligraphy. And whenever they traveled anywhere they were dependent on others taking them by rickshaw or carried by consorts in a sedan chair.

The practice of foot binding started with the wealthy class and eventually spread to the masses. It began falling out of use in the early 1900s, and after the People's Republic was formed in 1949, the practice was outlawed.

A few years after my marketplace education in Beijing, I was in the city of Kunming in southwest China. Kunming is a frontier town, a center for mountain tribal peoples, about 400 miles north of Hanoi, Vietnam. The Burma Road, built as a supply route during World War II, ended there. The city serves as a regional economic center for trade with Vietnam and Laos to the south, Burma to the west, and Tibet to the north.

Kunming, at 6000 feet above sea level, is known as the City of Eternal Spring because of its generously mild weather. Even in winter, the day will warm enough by afternoon so that a sweater and a scarf are enough to keep you warm.

One of my favorite places to visit in Kunming, to get away from the large Chinese crowds, is the Yuantong Buddhist Temple. It was built during the T'ang Dynasty, sometime between 600 and 900 A.D., a period of great freedom in art and religion throughout China.

The temple proper is painted a lacquered red that has aged with time. The ceiling is charred black from the centuries of incense smoke. As you enter the grounds through a heavy wooden Chinese gate, you are greeted by two giant white pines and a large stand of bamboo.

It was on a March afternoon that I saw the old woman walking along the path, a limestone trail that led past two carp filled ponds. It was a brilliant spring day, the marine blue sky looked so close that you had the feeling that you could reach up and grab the heavens above you. A soft wind rustled the bamboo leaves, as I strolled the grounds, my jacket in hand.

It was her lack of progress that I noticed first, as if a strong wind was keeping her from going forward. Then I looked down and saw the pointed five-inch shoes on her feet—handmade—embroidered with flowers and birds, a facsimile of the one's I had seen in Beijing.

The woman took very small steps and teetered in slow motion from side to side, like a penguin in high heels, a cane balancing her every movement.

In the instant that I made contact with the woman's brown eyes, the incredible history of China washed over me like a black cloud above the landscape. As a man, I somehow felt complicit in this woman's suffering, as if I was personally responsible for her pain.

"Women hold up half the sky," Mao exclaimed proudly in his *Little Red Book*. And yet in almost all cultures men set the rules, make the laws, and expect great, and often cruel and painful sacrifices from women.

Even under Mao's rule, the one child policy meant that a woman would often abort a female fetus in an effort to eventually deliver a baby boy, as a male heir would be expected to take care of his parents in their elder years—filial obligation from a culture that, for a thousand years, approved the breaking of the bones in a little girl's feet so that she would one day bring pleasure to a man.

I couldn't help but stare at the old woman as she walked in the afternoon sun toward the temple hall, knowing that I was seeing a macabre tradition from a long-ago time and place. It was as if history had stood still to let me peak in, to make of it what I would.

She strolled on as if in walking meditation, her body swinging like a pendulum keeping time. There was a reverence to her presence, like a prayer waiting to be offered.

2. Journey's End

Don Ronk died of a heart attack in Laos.

Don and I met when we worked together in a refugee camp for Vietnamese Boat People in the Philippines in the late 1980s. He was short and stocky with a wave of curly salt and pepper hair. The first time I met him, instead of saying hi, he said, "And what is it, pray tell, that you do around here?"

I laughed, which Don took as a sign that maybe I was alright after all.

Nancy, a mutual friend, gave me the news of Don's death. Don introduced the two of us after I moved to Hong Kong from the Philippines. He sent me a letter saying, "Hey big shot, you should meet my friend Nancy. Good people. Way smarter than you." The missive included her phone number.

Nancy, like Don, was an old Asia hand. She had just co-authored a book called *The Man with the Keys is Not Here* – a satirical piece about who got the blame when things went awry in communist China: the man with the keys, of course. It was his fault for opening the doors in the first place. The book was a big hit in British Hong Kong.

Don Ronk looked a lot like the actor Robert Mitchum, and like the actor was a chain smoking, hard drinking character. He sweet talked himself into a job in the camp. His bona fides included working as a war correspondent for the *Bangkok Post* in Laos and *San Francisco Chronicle* in Vietnam, before editing a magazine in Hong Kong. Prior to his work as a journalist, Don was a social worker. He headed the International Voluntary Services office in Da Nang from 1965 to 1967. He later resigned from IVS, along with three others, protesting in a letter to President Lyndon Johnson U.S. escalation of the war and its harmful effects on innocent Vietnamese people. The fact that he arrived in the Philippines by boat should have been a sign that Don was not your normal do-gooder. He liked to do things in his own unique way and abhorred the people in charge, which he displayed for all comers to see.

The camp, which housed 10,000 Vietnamese, was situated four hours north of Manila in Bataan province. Word was that Ferdinand Marcos located it there because he owed some favor to a crony who stood to benefit from a camp housing thousands of refugees being in the middle of nowhere. Subic Bay Naval base was a 20-minute drive up the coast through the jungle. The refugees, who spent six months being processed to go to the states, lived in small billets located in a series of neighborhoods. While they waited to go the U.S., the State Department sponsored English and various orientation classes to prepare them for entry into their new country. Most of them wanted to go to California.

By day, Don was a counselor in a middle school-like program for Amerasian teens—Vietnamese street kids who looked like Daddy from Kansas but spoke Vietnamese like Ho Chi Minh. They were confused, often unaccompanied, with a chip on their shoulder, having grown up as second-class citizens; visible reminders that the Yanks had wreaked havoc on their country.

At night, Don wandered the camp's interiors putting out fires and keeping the restless ones in line. To many people, Don was a crotchety old grouch who didn't like following orders, but to those of us who knew him, he was the grandpa with a soft spot that these kids warmed to.

It was in the camps that Don also met Vietnamese war veterans, most of whom had spent considerable time in prison after the war ended in 1975. They would sit in a makeshift café, sipping Vietnamese coffee while listening to Saigon pop music. Don listened to the men talk about their past lives, as well as their fears about their futures in America. Many of them had been in positions of leadership in the South Vietnam government and endured hardship in re-education camps, while their families were subject to a life of ridicule under the communist regime.

Don and I became even closer friends when we worked together on a formal study of these re-education prisoners in the camp, the problems they faced as second-class citizens in their post-war country. Many of them suffered from post-traumatic stress disorder and the study focused on the resettlement difficulties they would present in their new lives in America. The report later made the rounds of resettlement agencies in the US.

Don gave up flying after Vietnam. Riding in military choppers covering action in the field gave Don an uneasy feeling, especially after the helicopters he rode in kept getting shot at. After he left the refugee program, it took Don six months to find a transport on a ship from Manila to Hong Kong.

Soon after he arrived, I got a call from the Foreign Correspondents Club in Hong Kong. It was Don.

"Where the hell are you?" he asked.

By then Don had stopped drinking and was a mellower, gentler soul because of it. He would hold court with old friends, enemies and former colleagues, remembering their past lives when they were in the middle of the biggest news stories of their careers.

Don never considered returning to the states. He had been in Asia half of his adult life and had no intention of going back. I once passed a message to Don from Nancy that came from Don's son. It was in this indirect way that I first learned that Don had kin somewhere, that there had once been a woman in his life.

Don spent several months in Hong Kong and we would get together occasionally. But he didn't stay long. He took a boat trip to Shanghai and up the Yangtze. Then he found a boat to Thailand, where he crossed the Mekong and settled in Laos. Don and a Laotian partner set up a food stand selling Western-style cuisine, figuring that tourists would need something familiar after eating outside their comfort zone for a few days.

Laos was a quiet partner in the Vietnam conflict where the CIA enlisted Hmong tribesmen to fight against the communist insurgency. Don was one of the few journalists to write about what was being called The Silent War—a U.S. sponsored covert operation outside the purview of the American public. Surrounded by Vietnam, Thailand, Cambodia and China, the former monarchy couldn't escape the tide of change happening around them in Southeast Asia.

The Laos that Don returned to was a peaceful backwater with the war mostly forgotten, with people getting on with their lives.

"About the only ones in Laos who hurry are the tourists with backpacks, scuttling around looking for that dreamed-of free room and a meal, or quick-checking their guidebooks in the middle of the street to find out where they are," Don wrote to a mutual friend about the pace of life along the Mekong.

Laos abuts the Mekong river as it idles by on its way to the South China Sea. Landlocked and slow paced in a saffron-colored Buddhist kind of way, the once named Elephant Kingdom seemed the perfect place for Don to rest his bones, the kind of place where time slows down and journey's end. ◙

People lived here once
3 poems by Bart Sutter

Strange doings at Ross Elementary, 1956

When I was a kid on the Canadian border,
The grade school in the village there was plural—
Schools—because the farm folks roundabout
Had simply hauled in clapboard houses
On their flatbed trucks, set them on foundations
In a field, and hired teachers. Each teacher
Taught two grades, two grades per house,
Grades one through six, with one house left
To serve as cafeteria. They built a rink
With warming house, and, bingo, problem solved.

Everything was painted white because
The winters were so long no one could think
In any other color. The teachers helped us
Lace our skates for recess and called us
Back to work by standing on their porches
Swinging bells. Sometime along in May,
When ice had finally melted in the rink,
We cut rubber band boats out of plywood
And sent them puttering across the muddy ocean.
There were strange doings at that school. One day,
A classmate brought a flag for show-and-tell:
Scarlet, with a blue-and-white cross on its side.
This was the flag of Norway, and he'd fashioned it
To show that he was more than just American,
He was Norwegian, too. That flag inflamed us,
Made us crazed with jealousy, and we
Spent every recess chasing him while Norway
Fluttered in the wind he made by running wild.
That night, our houses stayed up late,
Brightened by the sound of bed sheets
Ripping and our humming as we colored them
And tacked the colors onto strips of lath.

Next day, the cloakroom bristled with our standards:
The red-and-white of Denmark, the sun-and-sky of Sweden,
The sky-and-snow of Finland, and Germany was there,
And Iceland looked like Norway inside out. At recess,
First and second graders of Ross Elementary
Burst from the schoolhouse like patriotic banshees

In high-speed parade, flags rippling in the breeze,
As we snaked around the schoolyard, ran
Full tilt, ecstatic, tears streaking from our eyes
Because the wind, because our grandparents,
Because we were carried away by who knows what.
A fundamental lesson in geography,
Phys. Ed., war, and just plain odd behavior
Which has lasted me my whole life long.

Lost locations

What happened to Norland, Grit, Pomme de Terre?
Once bustling towns, they're neither here nor there.
It upsets me when these days nobody talks
About berries near Pinecreek, Duxby, or Fox.
As a boy, I thought those hamlets would last forever.
It seems they've all gone the way of Belle River.

The ore was mined. The forest logged. Its function
Lost when the railway died, there went Winnipeg Junction.
What about Old Crow Wing, Mallard, and Moose,
Where people sold grog and used to chew snoose?
What happened to Darling, Dorothy, Hazel, Duane?
They had no importance. I miss them, just the same.
I do, and assume you do, too, though not many will,
Bewildered, keep asking the way to Gravelville
Or wonder out loud in the woods around Faunce,
"Where did they go? I heard how people lived here once."

I come from quiet people

I come from quiet people—
Norwegians, Swedes, and Danes. Oh, sure,
Women gossiped in the clash
Of silverware and dishes,
Cleaning up, and children might
Shout their happiness at finding frogs
Or scream at fingers pinched in doors.
I guess there was a man or two
Who liked to talk and joke—
Arden Bergen digging graves,
Ruddy-faced and sweaty, he was funny,
But a drainage ditch fell in on him,
So he went quiet years ago.

It helped to have a talker at a funeral
Or a wedding, but how many do you need?
The preacher made pronouncements
From the pulpit every Sunday, but
He was paid for that, then, wasn't he?
The men who shook his hand
When he stopped talking
Gathered in the furnace room
Or on the steps outside,
The smoke from cigarettes
Ascending into heaven like
The ghost of speculation held in check.

Politics might get them going,
The closing of a creamery,
But big talkers were considered
Entertainment, like the radio
Or clowns cavorting at the county fair.

What mattered there was showing up
When hay was down and skies were turning black.
What happened when a farmer fell into his silo
And drowned in all that grain
He'd worked so hard to store?
Would you dare to tell his widow you were *sorry*?
Better to come bearing casseroles
Like crucibles of frankincense and myrrh.

A white pine doesn't have too much to say,
And deer just gaze or bound away.
Rivers remember the ocean, but
They don't brag about it much
And only roar a couple times a year.
Have you noticed how the aspens quake
And natter nervously when clouds go sickly green?
Yet all their chatter never changed
The course of a tornado.

Here now, the Tingelstads
Just lost their farm and have to move to town.
What say you lift the far end of that table there?
Let's see if we can't hoist her in their truck.

The remarkable cat
Fiction by Daniel Moeller

Once upon a time there were three very happy cats. They lived in a cozy little house on the edge of a big woods. Their human friends, Vince and Jean, named them Athens, Sparta and Miss Annie. Athens and Sparta were named in honor of the famous cities of ancient Greece. Back then Athens was the center of culture, literature and philosophy. Citizens dressed in togas and debated the meaning of life. They asked why the sky was blue, the moon yellow and what their friends thought the winning lottery numbers would be.

Over in Sparta, they thought philosophy was all well and good, but other things were just as important. The Spartans were warriors. They needed to protect Greece from its enemies. What if 300,000 Persians suddenly showed up uninvited for dinner? Someone had to hold them off at the pass while the Athenians cooked something.

"This food is really good," said the Persians. "This food is to die for."

Spartan youth dressed for battle and practiced the military arts. They asked questions like "When can we go to war again?" What's your time in the marathon?" and "Has anybody seen my shield, it was here yesterday?"

Athens and Sparta, the cats, were a little like the cities they were named after. Athens was friendly and loving. He liked to sit on Vince or Jean's lap and purr. "Meow, meow." "Pet me," he was saying. "Rub my stomach."

Sparta was friendly too, but in his own way. He might sit on someone's lap, but only for a minute or two before he jumped off. Sparta was a big cat, the alpha male of the group. He enjoyed chasing Athens and Miss Annie around and around, just for the fun of it. Then they'd all take cat naps.

Sparta loved to prowl around the house, looking for interesting things to do. Was there a door he could open, maybe a forbidden space he could squeeze into? He never heard the saying, "Curiosity killed the cat." He was a feline *Dennis the Menace.* If Sparta had been a rabbit, he wouldn't have been Peter Cottontail hopping down the bunny trail. He would have been Peter Rabbit, with Mr. McGregor chasing him around his garden with a rake.

Sparta liked jumping up on the fireplace mantel. Maybe there was something up there he could knock over with his big paws or his bushy tail. After a while he would jump back down with a "meooooow." That meant, "look out below." Athens and Miss Annie went scurrying for cover.

Before long, Vince and Jean moved the big chair so Sparta couldn't jump on the fireplace mantel from it anymore. Then they put some of their favorite things on the mantel pierce. They thought they would be safe.

Sparta also loved jumping from the kitchen table to the top of the nearby kitchen shelf. "This can be your spot," said Jean, patting Sparta on the head. Sparta looked down to see Athens and Miss Annie, far below, starring up at him. He was the king.

One day, Sparta decided to jump from a kitchen counter to the top of the refrigerator. Before long he was reaching down and fiddling with the refrigerator magnets on the front. Soon, notes, pictures, recipes and the like were fluttering to the floor like snow.

"On my," said Jean when she came in the kitchen. She picked them all up and moved the magnets and their notes down the front of the refrigerator so Sparta couldn't reach them. "They look like the planes parked together in the center of the runway at Pearl Harbor to avoid sabotage," said Vince when he saw them. "We are trying to avoid sabotage," said Jean. "Sabotage by a Spartan."

Vince and Jean tried to keep Sparta from being too much like Peter Rabbit. They'd praise him when he was calm and give him treats. To give him exercise, they would buy cat toys like a giant mouse and a bird on a string and even a battery powered rabbit. It ran down before he did.

They bought a wand with a plastic cord on the ended. He loved to bat it around, first with one paw and the then the other. He looked like a prize fighter training for a bout. Then he'd try to bite it with his teeth. That's when Sparta looked the most ferocious.

Vince and Jean called that toy "the whip" because that's what it looked like. "I'm getting out the whip," Vince said to Jean one day.

"Oh, no, not the whip," Jean replied in an exaggerated, high pitched voice. "Not the whip. Anything but the whip. Please, not the whip."

"That's not what Sparta says," replied Vince, trying not to laugh. He knew Sparta loved "the whip."

His favorite toy, however, was Sparky, an old red beanie baby that Vince and Jean had. Sparta found it in a closet one day and began carrying it around in his teeth. Vince and Jean were amazed. Then Vince decided to see if Sparta would chase it and he threw it across the room. Sure enough, Sparta ran after it and carried it back to Vince in his mouth. When Vince threw it again, Sparta chased it and brought it back. After that, it became a game that Vince or Jean would play with him. They would throw Sparky and Sparta would chase it and bring it back.

"That cat must have some dog in him," said Jean. "I think so," said Vince. "Maybe he's a cog."

"Or he could be a dat," said Jean.

"He's not a feline," said Vince. "He's a fenine."

"Or maybe a caline," said Jean.

"No, Kaline was a Tiger," said Vince.

Jean looked at him and just shook her head and said "Huh?" she had never heard of the Detroit baseball player from years before.

Although Vince and Jean could joke about it, all that exercise with his toys only reduced Sparta's energy level by about, say, ten percent. Then Vince and Jean were forced to turn to negative reinforcement. They got little spray bottles filled with water. Whenever Sparta did something he shouldn't, Vince and Jean would blast him with a spray bottle. They stationed spray bottles in strategic spots around house. They looked like little silent sentinels guarding against enemy attack. They could have been Spartans themselves.

In truth, Sparta didn't really mind being blasted that much. He would run away, lick off the water, and before long, go right back doing what he had been doing.

"We need bigger spray bottles," Vince said to Jean one day.

"Yes, maybe we should get some super soakers," replied Jean.

"Maybe we should just bring in the hose," declared Vince.

He was kidding, of course, but not much.

Despite Sparta's antics, or maybe because of them, Vince and Jean really did love him. And he loved them.

However, here was one person who didn't love Sparta, or the other cats for that matter. It was Uncle George. George was Vince's brother but everybody called him Uncle George. Although he had many good qualities, love of cats wasn't one of them. He just didn't like cats. If Uncle George had been Noah, he would have let them behind.

"I don't understand why Uncle George doesn't like cats," Vince said to Jean. "We never had cats growing up so he's hardly been around them. The only cats he really sees are when he comes to visit. Then there's just Miss Annie, Athens, and ...."

Vince stopped his thought. "Oh, I guess I know why he doesn't like cats," said Vince.

"Well," said Jean, "Sparta is rambunctious, but he's loveable. And he wouldn't hurt a fly."

"Uncle George isn't a fly," said Vince. "I think he's afraid of Sparta."

Vince remembered the last time Uncle George came for a visit. They were talking about cats. "The only good cat," said Uncle George, is a …"

Well, you know the rest of the sentence.

"Don't say that," said Vince. "They'll hear you."

"Don't be silly," said Uncle George. "Cats can't understand us."

"They understand more than you think," said Vince.

"Oh, brother," said George.

Later, Uncle George was relaxing in the big chair telling Vince and Jean what a great time he was having. Then Sparta entered the room. Uncle George stopped talking and stared at Sparta. The cat began walking around and around Uncle George's chair like a fox might circle a henhouse. Uncle George eyed Sparta with suspicion the way a lamb chop would eye a wolf if it could. Then Sparta did a strange thing, he jumped right up onto Uncle George's lap. George tensed up. He didn't pet Sparta, he didn't talk to him. He just looked straight ahead. He was both shocked and uncomfortable. Finally, Sparta jumped down and went away.

"I guess he likes you," said Vince.

"Yes," said Uncle George. "The same way a kid likes an ice cream cone. The ice cream cone loses in the end."

Miss Annie was Vince and Jean's female cat. She was Jean's favorite. One day while walking in the woods, Jean heard a faint meowing. Jean followed the sound and found a little kitten all alone. She was hungry and cold. "Meow," she said. "Meow. Meow." That meant, "feed me," help me." "Take me home."

And that's just what Jean did. She became Miss Annie.

Vince and Jean called her "the beautiful and haughty Miss Annie."

She was beautiful, nothing like the bedraggled creature Jean had found in the woods. She was a wonderful mix of brown, black and even gray fur. As a bonus, the end of each paw was a lovely white color. "She's the most beautiful cat in the world," said Jean. It seemed that Miss Annie knew she was beautiful. Like a beautiful lady, she could afford to be particular. She would never crawl up on Jean's lap. Instead, she was curl up in a nearby chair. With one eye open, she would watch the rest of her family just to see what they were doing. She would especially be on alert in case Sparta and Athens came racing up to her. Then they would run around until they all got tired and decided to take naps.

Well, Sparta was chasing Athens and Miss Annie around the house one day. They raced down a hallway and into the living room, lickety-split. Then Sparta saw it. Someone had moved the chair closed to the fireplace. Sparta knew he could make the leap now. Like a racecar driver at Indianapolis heading to the pits, he veered off from chasing Athens and Miss Annie and went straight for the chair. In a second, he jumped onto it and then onto the mantelpiece going as fast as he could. He had never done that before. Sparta landed on the mantel with a thud and started to slide on the shiny marble. He careened along the mantel, knocking over Vince and Jean's wedding picture. Then he toppled a picture of Jean's mother, and for good measure, upset a photo of Vince's dad. All went plummeting onto the hard bricks of the hearth below. Finally, at the far end of the mantel was a framed plaque Jean had received for being her school's teacher of the year. Sparta tried to stop with all his might, but he couldn't. Bang. He crashed into the prize award and it went flying as well. Then Sparta slid off the edge of the mantelpiece and fell toward the floor himself. He had to use one of his nine lives just to land safely on the carpet.

The things he knocked off weren't so fortunate. Sparta looked around. Cracked picture frames and pieces of glass lay all about him. It was not what he expected just seconds before. "Meow," he said, which meant, "Oh no," and he headed for a hiding place under his favorite chair.

Athens and Miss Annie, looked at the mess, meowed and scampered away as well. Then all was quite in the living room.

Meanwhile, Vince and Jean were outside, happily tending their garden. They didn't hear all the commotion inside. When they finished and walked into the living, they got an unpleasant surprise. "Mother," gasped Jean when she saw mother's picture. "Dad," said Vince. "Us," they both said when they saw their smashed wedding picture. "My award," exclaimed Jean, rounding out the list of destruction.

"SPARTA," Vince and Jean yelled together.

"Where is that cat?" said Jean.

"I'll get the hose," said Vince. Now Jean for sure couldn't tell if he was kidding.

Sparta watched from under his chair. He was trying to make himself as small as possible. He no longer felt like a king. He felt like a peasant. In dramatic lore, kings stand and face adversity, but peasants don't have to fight. Sparta saw his chance and bolted for the stairs. Once upstairs, he hid under a bed. There, Sparta told himself he might never come out.

While Sparta hid upstairs, Vince and Jean cleaned up the broken frames and pieces of glass. Somehow their wedding picture had a big crease right down the middle, separating the two newlyweds.
"I didn't know we were going to split like this," said Vince.

"It was pretty sudden," replied Jean.

"Your dad is really showing his age," said Jean, looking at that damaged picture with lines running through it.

"Your mom has looked better herself," replied Vince. After that, they both laughed. They stopped being so mad at Sparta.

Upstairs, Sparta didn't know they were laughing. He stayed under the bed. Finally, he fell asleep. As the poet said, "to sleep, perchance to dream." Sparta liked dreaming. Sometimes he dreamt that he was outside chasing birds and rabbits. Sometimes he dreamt that Jean gave him his favorite kind of cat food. And sometimes he dreamt that he climbed up a high tree and the fire department had to come and rescue him. That was fun.

The dream that Sparta had that day wasn't fun however. It was a cat nightmare. First, Vince and Jean started yelling at him. "Bad cat," "Naughty cat," they said. Then they started chasing him around the house with their spray bottles, trying to blast him. Next, the rest of the spray bottles grew legs, and ran after him too. Finally, Athens and Miss Annie joined in the chase. Sparta darted here and there, looking for an open door or an open window, someplace to escape his pursuers, but he found none. Finally, just when it seemed he couldn't run anymore, he woke up.

He opened his eyes and there were Miss Annie and Athens starring at him. "Meow," said Miss Annie, which meant, "you made a mess."

"Meow, Meow," said Athens. "You're going to get it." Then they walked away.

Sparta stared out at the empty bedroom. He felt all alone. Then he went back to sleep. This time he didn't dream.

When he awoke, the sun was going down. Sparta stood up and felt something. It was a hunger pain. "Time for supper," he thought to himself. Sparta sniffed to see if he could smell the aroma of cat food drifting up from the downstairs. He did smell something but it wasn't food. It was, it was smoke!

Sparta went out into the hall and smelled again. It was stronger this time. He looked at ceiling where the trap door was that led to the antic. Vince or Jean could yank on a little chain that pulled down the stairs that went to the attic. Sparta had only been up once. That's when Vince and Jean were up there looking for things they called antiques. While they explored, he explored. Before long he was covered with little bits of attic insulation and a whole bunch of cobwebs. After that, Vince and Jean never let him come back up there.

Sparta looked at the door and saw little whiffs of smoke coming out from a small crack in it. Fire! Sparta knew he had to do something. He ran downstairs and right up to Vince and Jean who were in the living room.

"Bad cat," said Jean when she saw him. "Go away," said Vince and he frowned at Sparta.

Then Sparta began doing what he did best. He began running around. He ran around and around Vince and Jean. Then he bolted back upstairs. The smell was stronger. He ran back down and circled the room hoping Vince or Jean would notice him.

"What is with that cat?" asked Jean. "I don't know," said Vince as he grabbed for a spray bottle.

Athens and Miss Annie watched to see what would happen next.

"Meow," said Sparta. That meant, "Chase me. Chase me."

Miss Annie just watched haughtily but Athens sensed something was wrong. "Meow," he said and began chasing Sparta. Around they ran, the two cats. Then Sparta raced upstairs and Athens followed. When he got upstairs Athens stopped. He smelled the smoke too and saw it coming from the attic. "Meoow!" he said. Then both cats raced downstairs. Sparta charged past Vince and Jean with Athens in quick pursuit. Then he ran to the foot of the stairs and stopped and so did Athens. They were inviting Vince and Jean to follow them. Next, they ran halfway up the stairs and stopped. The two cats named for ancient city states seemed to have joined forces to defeat a common enemy just like the Greeks of old. They had to warn Vince and Jean. When Miss Annie saw how excited Sparta and Athens were, she finally decided to join in too and ran to the stairs as well.

"That's strange said Vince. "I think they want us to follow them," said Jean. Vince and Jean started up the stairs. As they got to Sparta and Athens and Miss Annie, the three cats ran up the rest of the way upstairs and into the hall. Vince and Jean followed. "Fire," said Vince, only he didn't meow.

He pulled the door leading to the attic down and more smoke shot out. He could see orange flames too. Vince grabbed a fire extinguisher from their bedroom and turned in on the fire. They would need more than that, he realized. "Call the fire department, I'll get the hose," said Vince. He ran outside, grabbed the hose lying by the front door and dragged it inside. It was the first time he had actually brought the hose in the house. When he got upstairs, Jean turned on the water. Vince pointed the hose at the attic and trained the water on the fire. All his practice of blasting Sparta with spray bottles was finally paying off. Soon, the fire started dying down. By the time the fire department arrived, it was out. There was some water and smoke damage in the attic but it could have been a lot worse.

"How did it start?" asked Jean.

"It was probably electrical," said the fire chief. "It was lucky you found out about the fire when he did. "How did you notice it?"

"Our cats smelled it," said Jean. "They alerted us."

"Fire cats, now I've heard of everything," said the chief. "I bet you are proud of them."

"We sure are," said Vince.

After the firefighters left, Vince and Jean went through the house and rounded up all the spray bottles. They emptied them and put them away in a closet.

"We don't need these anymore," said Vince.

"No," said Jean. "Not when we have a cat like Sparta."

"Don't forget Athens and Miss Annie," said Vince.

"Meow," said Sparta. "Meow," said Athens. "Meow," said Miss Annie.

"You're right," all three of them seemed to be saying. Then they went into the kitchen and Jean gave them a big bowl of cat food. It tasted wonderful. Then the three cats fell asleep and Sparta dreamed about his big adventure. He felt like a king again. ◉

Pairs
Poems by sisters Connie Sanderson & Nancy Kay Peterson

Editor's Note: A sampler from the unpublished manuscript, *Parings/Pairings: Poems between Sisters*. Connie Sanderson, elder sister to Nancy Kay Peterson, is now deceased.

Graphic from an original 1976 print, *Pears*, by Jane Miller

Apology to Jean Gill

You lay on the garage floor helpless,
unable to get back into the chair,
its silver wheels glinting
in late afternoon light.
Two stumps of legs

lost to World War II
flailed like caught fish.
Your strong arms struggled
to pull you back up,
but the wheels would not stand still.

I watched motionless, invisible,
too small to help. I should have
run home for my father
but was too embarrassed
for you and for me.

WWII Vet

They lined up
shoulder to shoulder
on summer evenings,
all four men from
the neighborhood houses,
taking turns throwing
a baseball to Jean.
We kids shagged his misses,
a ruse to be useful and
stay outside longer,
excited to *"toss one
in the ol' breadbasket,"*
Jean's big soft tummy.
His old glove was faded,
worn smooth from the impacts
of thousands of balls.
We never thought about
how he might have felt
using that old keepsake
to catch pitches from
his neighbors and their kids,
him in his tee shirt and shorts,
sitting in his chair,
no legs below his knees.

Connie Sanderson

Nancy Kay Peterson

Grandfather's favorite cousin
for Janna Banngren

The sun was shining in Oslo
the day I visited you
for the first and last time.
Your tiny apartment was always
the beginning of Grampa's visits
to the old country he loved.

We interwove our languages
so we could nearly understand
each other among the bric-a-brac
of your eighty years. My twenty-
something life had just begun.
Before I left you gave me

a traditional rosemalled bowl.
Then into my hand you pressed
a tiny wood rabbit, painted white,
poised on a four-leaf clover.
I think your wink meant
it was a fertility charm.

Thirty years and an ocean away,
married but childless too,
I lift this talisman
from my dresser drawer,
think of you and how our lives
sometimes go on despite us.

Scandinavian white on black
*(Betsy Moen, Mary Bohn, Julia Bergen, Nettie Moen,
Emma Severson, Inger Peterson, Anna Johnson)*

Seven sisters,
a string of paper dolls,
gaze at distant mystery.

Seven stoic faces
framed by swept-back hair,
pinned in proper place.

Seven floor-length dresses,
long-sleeved, cinch-waisted,
scant on lace and ruffles.

Seven prim high collars,
three held by ribbons,
two closed by cameos.

One mouth, pinch-lipped,
set and sour. One head
tilted at a jaunty angle.

Another's chin held high.
One face, moon-round, sparkles.
The next one draws back, wary.

One set of eyes
writ soft with sorrow,
one timid set, downcast.

Seven sisters'
passings held
in silver silence.

One camera's eye
can't show their paths
to seven separate graves.

Connie Sanderson

Emily Dickinson explains

I wore white because
it was the thing to wear
to reflect all hues
that came to me.

White is simple—
simpler than the poems
that rushed from my pen.
Once descending the stairs

I froze, became a tableau
against the mirror—
against the world I thought
would never claim me for its own.

I climbed the stairs to my room
collapsed at the writing table
laid down my head and wept
for the loneliness of everyone.

Nancy Kay Peterson

Not Emily Dickinson

She read her poem,
a bad poem,
and followed it with another.

It was a cool Sunday afternoon.
She was dressed in her Midwest best,
fuzzy design sweater, polyester pants.

Her smiling husband, in a brand-new shirt,
had driven her two-and-a-half hours,
all the way from Saint somewhere,

so she could join this open class
to read her poems in a wheezy voice,
the pages rattling in her quaking hands.

At the end of the last cliché, she looked
to the instructor with such desperation,
we were embarrassed by her naked need.

We all knew her poems weren't very good,
knew the devastation of her knowing
was a brink she could not cross.

Her husband sat there proud and happy,
believing in his wife, unaware
of the judgments swirling about her,

and the instructor smiled stiffly,
thanked her very much for reading,
and said everything expected,

except the truth.

Connie Sanderson   Nancy Kay Peterson

At the Cranberry Museum

Being a cranberry is more complicated
than it looks. You grow in sand beds

which can be sprinkled or flooded to prevent
stress from heat or damage from frost.

Sometimes a bee shortage prevents pollination.
Foreign bees are imported and put into service.

To simplify harvest, you must learn to float.
Inner air pockets become life preservers.

Once picked you get seven chances to bounce
over
four-inch rails. If you fail, you're rejected

not good enough for human consumption
in sauces or jellies, juices or candies

not good enough for museum shop candles
not good enough for sachet or soap.

At the Cranberry Museum

Imagine your life was a museum.
Historical markers marked where you lived.
Towns would claim you as a native son (or
daughter).
There would be those mysterious lost years
when no one knows what you did. (Nothing.)
They'd display the desk you wrote at,
your pen. (They'd search for your revisions.)

Imagine your life was a museum,
everything just as you had left it.
Would your underwear drawer be neat and tidy?
Would the book you'd been reading be open to
that page,
or would they have to re-create everything from
scratch,
confess to re-enactment, try to find an old lava
lamp,
black and white TV, old toaster, silly putty?

Would your death be an exhibit, too?
The how, the why, the site you died?
Would they charge admission to your grave?
Would reverent people bring you flowers?
Imagine your life was a museum.
Would you live it differently?

Connie Sanderson

Night chant

When our lives are all we have,
wind softly lifts each curtain,
and sleep erases sorrow
as fireflies pulse outside.

Wind softly lifts each curtain.
Clouds drift across the moon.
As fireflies pulse outside,
we dream of one another.

Clouds drift across the moon.
The river flows towards seas.
We dream of one another,
but no river runs forever.

The river flows towards seas
as it hums beneath our dreams,
but no river runs forever.
Even love can change.

As it hums beneath our dreams,
we turn to one another.
Even love can change.
Shadows bathe our bodies.

We turn to one another.
Blood rests between each heartbeat.
Shadows bathe our bodies.
We can barely wait for morning.

Blood rests between each heartbeat,
and sleep erases sorrow.
We can barely wait for morning
when our lives are all we have.

Nancy Kay Peterson

Universality

Within a universe both cruel and kind,
when Pachelbel's sweet, sighing Canon plays,
your olive face, unbidden, comes to mind.

Where chaos is the heart of grand design,
two orbits touching set the skies ablaze
within a universe both cruel and kind.

In music, art and poetry I find
I hear your laughter, see your almond gaze;
your olive face, unbidden, comes to mind.

Our strands of time, in harmony combined,
will last as long as nights turn into days
within a universe both cruel and kind.

And, now each day, although I am resigned
to choosing lives demanding separate ways,
your olive face, unbidden, comes to mind.

Please think of me as though we're still entwined.
My thoughts of you, my friend, shine through
time's haze.
Within a universe both cruel and kind,
your olive face, unbidden, comes to mind.

Judy Garland's mother
by Konnie Ellis

I ran into Nancy Lee in the *NorShor Theater* in Duluth, Minnesota. It had been some years since we had seen each other, and I was embarrassed that I couldn't recall her name. It seemed inexcusable, like forgetting one's sister's name. After all, we had been roommates for a summer during our college years, and I certainly hadn't forgotten her. She used to sit out on the balcony on warm summer evenings with her guitar and sing Joan Baez songs, her voice as clear and true as a nightingale's. She crooned, she crowed, she howled like a Ginsberg angel, back in those days of our youth. She always seemed to be in another dimension out there on the balcony, completely alone and at the same time part of the night, part of nature like some odd fallen star that had landed on a campus apartment balcony in Minneapolis, Minnesota, quite by chance, and had decided to stay and sing a song or two.

The old renovated theater seemed an appropriate place to run into her again, with its expansive art deco interior, high ceilings with chandeliers, plush turquoise carpet with bright zigzags and twirls, and a wide circular staircase dramatic enough for a Betty Davis entrance. A tall, attractive man accompanied Nancy Lee. He had a notable head of wavy blond hair, and stood in the shadows like a man who just moments before had stepped down from an old movie poster and was not yet quite ready for real life. Nancy Lee and I exchanged telephone numbers at the top of the staircase, then went our separate ways as a fresh batch of popcorn popped in the lobby.

One week later, Nancy Lee and I are standing beside a house that looks like it could tip over. The support from one corner has been removed, leaving a fourth of the house perched above a pit of fresh dirt. This is the house where Judy Garland's mother lived when she worked as a seamstress. She lived on the second floor. Nancy Lee has always known things like this, unusual things hardly anyone else knows about, so I'm not surprised to be standing by the lilacs next to this pile of dirt outside Judy Garland's mother's house. Nancy Lee starts right up the old metal fire escape stairs. I follow. On the second story landing, I am wary. Close up, this house looks really old. A metal ledge circles the back of the house and is wide enough to walk upon, but is it strong enough to hold us up, to hold us both up? She marches right out onto the platform. I venture out one step, barely putting my weight down—a ballerina's step, or a coward's step. Nancy Lee is heavier than I am, and I hear no buckling of the metal, so I follow cautiously while she talks about Judy Garland's mother.

"Her name was Ethel. I know, very old-fashioned, but probably a very cool name in 1912. Anyway, Ethel played the piano for silent movies, and got a job at the Savoy Theater over in Superior. Judy was the youngest, born in Grand Rapids. This house was moved from its original location down by the courthouse," she adds, but doesn't know when.

I saw an advertisement in last week's *Budgeteer News* for the Judy Garland Festival up in Grand Rapids, but I think this is more fun, partly because it's more dangerous, and partly because it's like our own small festival, and besides, it's free. We stop at the windows and peer inside. The rooms are empty, and most noticeable are the wooden floors, beautiful wooden floors with soft afternoon rectangles of light from the windows, a wooden floor with any number of possibilities. Here you could dance, do yoga, meditate in the middle of a beautiful oriental rug of many colors. We are both silent, contemplating the floor. Judy Garland's mother's floor. Ethel's floor. She might have kept her sewing machine over by those tall windows so she could enjoy the squirrels in the trees while she worked. It would have been one of those heavy oak and steel machines decorated with gold arabesques, with little drawers for buttons and bobbins, and a foot peddle for propulsion. She might have had a piano against that long inner wall by the bedroom.

The silence of the empty apartment makes the wind in the trees seem loud, and I think of contemporary silence, as when the electricity goes off and one is startled by a sudden emptiness—as when Thomas Hampson's voice from a CD stops mid-phrase and you listen carefully to the quiet trying to figure out what is missing besides the music—the hum of a refrigerator? The drone of a TV? I imagine Ethel working in her quiet apartment, the only sound the rhythmic peddling of the sewing machine treadle. Perhaps she hears the iceman's horse pass by, its hoofs clicking dependably down an unpaved road. Or she might be at an old upright piano, slightly out of tune: *Brother can you spare a dime?*

Did Judy Garland's mother laugh in this very room. Dance? What did it smell like in the kitchen? Did she bake raisin cookies? Did she sit in that little kitchen and eat oatmeal and sip coffee on chilly Duluth mornings? Did she smoke? Could there be a cowardly lion in the broom closet? Nancy Lee is as quiet as I am. She looks lost in thought too. Maybe she is picturing Liza Minelli, all glittered up and ready to go on stage in Cabaret, rehearsing here in a dream, sashaying around on the wooden floor of the empty room, fluttering her lashes and sighing theatrically. Or perhaps she is thinking of her own mother, who was a professional dancer, dancing on floors like this. The empty apartment with its wooden floors is so full of promise and mystery that we lean toward the windows expectantly, as if for a play about to begin, or continue.

You can see Lake Superior from out here on the ledge, though you probably couldn't see the lake from inside, or perhaps just a bit from the kitchen. My mother wasn't allowed to take dancing lessons because my grandmother considered dancing not quite proper, and in the same category as black net stockings. Decadent. But my mother's best friend Jean Gronseth took lessons, and after class taught my mother the steps in Gronseth's green garage on Skyline Parkway. My mother can tap, Charleston, waltz, anything. She has a natural talent. She could even walk on her hands. Both she and Jean Gronseth could do that. We leave the window and Nancy Lee sits down on the roof ledge facing the lake. I unfold a scarf to sit on. We each have an orange to peel. We stare out at the lake like old men sitting in rocking chairs on their porch, peeling oranges and rocking, deep in thought, and absentmindedly content. A ship is nearing the harbor but is still quite far off. Out above the lake in the watery blue sky, I picture my mother walking on her hands, a Chagall-like figure walking along a cloud, occasionally flipping upright to do the Charleston. Maybe Nancy Lee sees her mother dancing out there too, all dressed up, sophisticated and glamorous, instead of how she really is now, in a nursing home. On a roof you can see things, put things in perspective. These oranges have nice thick peels, and I eat some of the white. The orange oil is pleasant in the air and I can smell the lilacs in the yard below. Next door the deep red peonies are just beginning to open.

"A penny for your thoughts," I say, surprised that I'm using such a dumb cliché.

"God," Nancy Lee says and laughs her complicated laugh of many syllables, a laugh like a poem, or at the least, a Haiku. A boat whistle blows, long and low. We watch the aerial bridge rise slowly.

"Have you seen the dancers who dance on the bridge?" I ask, and tell her my visits are usually just before or after that performance. She's seen them, she tells me, and it's like they're flying above the bridge, above the water like bright mythical birds, and the seagulls come too, and swoop up and down so the dancers and the birds are all choreographed together and it's quite wonderful, with the music and the squawking. I want the music to be Mozart's Magic Flute and I think of it over the water and here on the roof. Now, what to do with the orange peels. My friends the Keatses had shrimp with Mrs. Dylan Thomas once and sat by an open window, throwing their shrimp peelings out the window. Ever since I've wanted to do that. But I would feel like a litterbug, tossing down the orange peels here in Duluth.

"You're having a dilemma," Nancy Lee says, watching me puzzle over the orange peels. "Use your purse." I do as she says. The boat passes under the bridge and into the harbor. An ore boat.

"During the war my dad saw a man fall into a giant vat of molten steel," I tell her, the most violent image I know of.

"That's sick, telling me that is just sick."

"I know," I confess. "It's because of the peels, not knowing what to do with them. Not knowing." She looks at me for a while, Buddha like, and I can feel my aura being analyzed.

"I think you should meet Andreas," she tells me after some time. "Andreas has been so reclusive though, for the past ten years he's been terribly terribly reclusive." She shakes her head slowly.

Just like me I think, but make no comment. Now the bridge is down.

"I like this apartment," Nancy Lee says. "It feels good; it feels right."

"Did you ever ride on the bridge when it was going up?" I ask.

"You can't do that," she says. "You can't do that." She looks so stern. I tell her I did it as a kid—that I was so skinny I could lie down flat and no one even saw me go up, that I heard the cables squeak after the warning bells rang, and I went straight up with the bridge and stayed up too, turning onto my stomach to look down through steel mesh to the water below and I watched the ship from South America come right through, the big white ship that carried coffee, floating over the blue water below, the most beautiful ship in the world, and I saw it all from the bridge when I was only ten, and then the bell rang again, and the bridge came back down. That was back when the bridge was black, before they painted it silver white, I noted, as if that made it riskier, more dangerous.

"It *was* black," she says.

"Well," I sigh. After a long pause I ask if she knows that bridge over by Leif Erickson park that's made of dark granite. She does. I tell her how we used to stand on that bridge after Sunday School. We would stand in its curved center and wait for the train. It felt like you were standing on top of a thick castle wall because you couldn't see the opening below for the train to pass through; instead it looked like the train would crash into the wall you were standing on. When the noisy smoky black train got close I would scream and run off the bridge. My brother David, on the other hand, stayed on the bridge the whole time. I admired that. I always admired my brother.

"I'm sure I'd run too. I'd scream and run." Nancy Lee laughs. "Usually I'm not a runner though. I let things come."

"You're a rock," I tell her.

"Granite.

"Coal."

"Lodestone."

"I could be a rock, probably," I say. "Sandstone perhaps. Or on my best days, amber. Well, that's not exactly a rock . . ."

"Lapis Lazuli. Lake Superior blue. Cold." Nancy Lee says, and pretends to shiver.

I like the way she pronounces Lapis Lazuli. Carefully, dramatically: La-shu-lie.

"Lapis Lazuli," I repeat. I'm feeling happy now, the sun has come out and we're in a cheerful sunny spot on this roof.

"She didn't sing too well—Judy Garland's mother. Ethel. It was her father who had the voice. They met in Superior." Nancy Lee lies back on the roof, setting an orange peel on each eye.

"Remember that time you called me up and then sang every number from Carmen on the phone?" I ask.

"No. Well, yes," she laughs, rearranging the peels. "I needed a preview. I was a very good Carmen. You should have seen me." She kicks out a plump leg.

I like being on the roof. It's fun, being up high like this. "Anyway, why did they do Carmen? I mean Carmen is so un-Minnesotan."

She doesn't appear to be listening, but I don't mind. She's humming her Carmen role. Suddenly she gets up and rushes across the rooftop ledge, calling to me that she'll be right back.

Maybe she will, maybe she won't. She might forget or be distracted. As she leaves I watch two sail boats out on the lake. It's Wednesday, sailboat day. It must be too rough or there would be more. I settle back to enjoy the boats, and note the whitecaps off Park Point, my mind relaxed and bobbing pleasantly, like the waves.

The fire stairs shake as Nancy Lee rushes back up the stairs and stomps over the roof ledge. "I called Andreas," she says. "He's waiting for a truck. His marble is coming in a Mayflower truck."

"Oh, that's right, he's an artist. I had forgotten. Somehow I thought he was one of your poets." She sees I notice the bottle of wine sticking out of her jumper pocket.

"Madeira. I bought it yesterday. I don't drink anymore, so I bought Madeira."

She may be apologizing with her eyebrows, or expressing excitement. I can't tell. But it seems classy, sipping Madeira on the roof of Judy Garland's mother's house. We should have wine glasses though. I decide to go look for some in the empty apartment, if I can get in. Nancy Lee settles down on the roof and I'm off on my wine glass mission. The back door is locked and there are storm windows on all the windows, except for a kitchen window, which I can't get up. It's either locked or stuck. I use the file on my nail clipper as a lever, and the window slides up. This is fun I decide as I climb through the window. I brush aside the dead flies on the window ledge and ease myself down to the floor. Inside it smells like wood shavings and lemon, at least at first, until I sniff something that makes me think of old magazines and sprouted potatoes. Stepping on the actual floor gives me a genuine thrill. The sun on the floor really does emphasize the emptiness of the apartment and I automatically raise my hand to my heart and take a deep breath. I bend down, prepared to study the scuff marks on the floor of Judy Garland's mother's house. These marks on the floor have meaning. I stare as I sometimes do at Vincent van Gogh paintings, noting the strokes, thinking that Vincent stood in front of this very canvas and made that very mark. These marks. These foot marks on the floor. I shuffle around the kitchen as if I have some affliction, or am waiting until my feet start dancing of their own accord. Then I get to business and open the cupboards one after the other. All empty except for old newspaper lining. Luckily though, the pantry is filled with canning jars. I remove the lids from two, put one in my purse and hold one in my hand as I climb back out, politely shutting the window behind me.

Almost gleeful with the wine glasses, even if they're only canning jars, I settle down on the roof, ready to celebrate. Nancy Lee pours the Madeira into the pale green glass jars. I had forgotten how sweet it is. Sweet like brandy, and there's something grandmotherly about it. We sit on the roof of the empty house and sip wine like we are the most aristocratic of the aristocrats. You would think Nancy Lee was Queen Elizabeth she's so dignified.

"Tell me about your poets," I say.

"Well, there weren't that many," she says. "Just a few. A few poets is enough. One would be enough actually."

"I had one once," I tell her. "One poet."

"Yes?"

"He slipped away."

"Ah. Yes, they do that, one way or another, they slip away."

"Look, there's the truck! The Mayflower. That might be Andreas' marble."

We watch the big truck go east along Superior Street, excited as kids watching the ice cream truck, and we totally forget our recent exaggerated dignity.

"Tell me about his sculpture," I say.

"Egg shapes. And bone shapes. Very sensual," she tells me.

I pour us each another glass.

"Look, more sailboats going out. So tiny."

"Sail away to Jesus," Nancy Lee belts out like a southern gospel heavy weight. "Sail away . . ."

I finish my Madeira, wondering how many birds she just woke up, and I feel dizzy as I look out over the lake, surprised that the sun is beginning to set. My legs feel long and stretched out dangling over the roof ledge and I retrieve the orange peels from my purse and toss one over the ledge. It's pleasant, watching an orange peel flutter down through the air.

"Van Gogh," I say as I toss the second peel.

"Kandinsky," Nancy Lee says, helping herself to several of my peels.

"Van Gogh's brother," I say tossing the longest peel.

"Kandinsky's grandmother. And all the rest of them, Andreas too," Nancy Lee says as she tosses the last of her peels with a flourish.

We laugh, and the metal of the roof kind of shakes. Nancy Lee slaps it with her hand and it makes an echoing sort of reverberation. "The house is laughing," she says. "Are we drunk?" she asks seriously.

"No. We're just a bit off." I tell her. We decide to climb down while we can, and carefully.

On the fire stairs we decide to do this again someday.

"Someday soon. Next Tuesday?" Nancy Lee suggests.

"But I leave for Denver tomorrow," I say.

"Ah well. Life. Always ends with unfinished business," she says matter-of-factly. We go our separate ways, each settling a green glass canning jar into the beverage holder of our respective cars. As we drive away from the house we toot our horns, like two seasoned tugboats ready to chug right along into the future, come rain or come shine. ◎

Nathan Wagoner
Solve for x

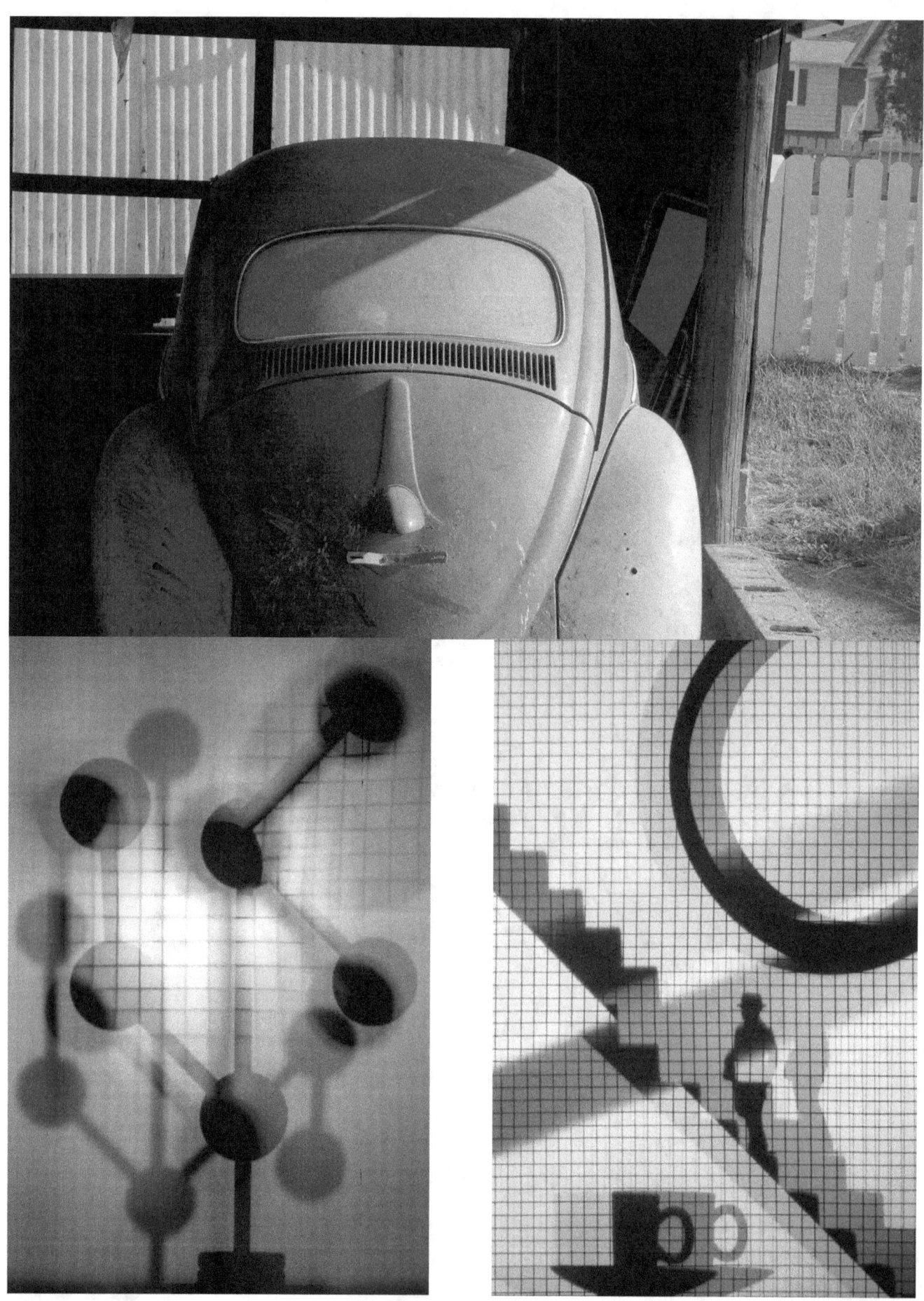

A wise fool's song
4 poems by Robert Wooten

An Ogdoad

One denotes an anteriority of nonexistence.
Psychology begins with number two; three, the number
of platonic reality, which excludes the fallen;
four, the number of the quaternity, a number
of inclusive reality, encompassing time, as with four
directions, seasons, Gospels; five, the physical man;
six—the fallen; seven, the number of angels, eight,
a number of nonoccurrence and preexistent totality.

Negredo

That dark wood of Scots,
of undoing in then and there,
as if I were upside down
with some One there, in an alchemical way,
and with this and that to choose
between, each as a course of action:
In the bell of the giganticus,
one cannot choose. Anything that large
has its own center of gravity.
And I was reduced to knowing
this from that, quite apart
from a doable outcome. It was not
what I wanted: Each there
had a Scot at the other end
begging to differ. And then, I found myself
at antipodes. I knew this could be
the effect of an other. It was called
Mary, Queen of Scots, "scot"
meaning "dim." I could see nothing
in another's dim view but a point of contention.

The man of light

In a blind man's eyes,
stars burn here.
It is night, bright stars.
Now, it is morning,
a pain in my head,
and, in the cupboard,
moldy bread,
dim constellations

overhead.
And, outside, the rain,
then, inside, the house,
in hiding, in pain,
a wise fool's song.

The star

The night has been so lonely,
so lonely.

And so,
   for a puzzle to fit the ends we make
of ourselves,
   we construct more ships
to sail.
And, always, we hope,
though blackest night wrap its talons round
our hearts,
to glimpse the aura,
to catch sight of some star, or harbor.
But we look for ourselves.
   And the rest? To hell . . .

so find the objects that through shadows
(so Shallow) throw darkness on our souls.

The afternoon lies heavily
   through the windows of my room.
Is there such a place as a high window?

I hear the shadows crawling in.
Another day, at long last,
has walked in single file
and come to pass.

The night has been so lonely.
Perhaps, I hear it pass.

WWII survivor still wonders, 'Why me?'
By John Weiss

From **Back Roads** (*Lost Lake Folk Art* & *The Rochester Post Bulletin*, 2017)

Paul Ness served as a Navy Sonarman in WWII

I t's been seventy years since World War II ended, but Paul Ness continues to ask, "Why? Why me?"

He and fellow 1939 Spring Valley High School graduates Rodney Weeks and Ray Hatlestad volunteered at the same time to join the Army Air Force. They wanted to fly fighter planes.

He and fellow 1939 Spring Valley High School graduates Rodney Weeks and Ray Hatlestad volunteered at the same time to join the Army Air Force. They wanted to fly fighter planes.

"I wanted to serve my country," Ness said. Weeks and Hatlestad were accepted, but Ness was rejected because his blood pressure wouldn't drop fast enough. Instead, he joined the Navy.

His two friends were killed, he still lives.

"I was lucky. My classmates were killed and I'm still living. How come?" he asked.

In his Spring Valley home, Ness has a picture of Richard Dormady, who grew up on a neighboring farm north of Spring Valley. He was killed when his ship took a direct hit from a bomb. Why?

A really good boxer whom Ness sparred with in the service was leading a patrol when a sniper shot him. By then, Ness had been shipped home. "I feel God took care of me," he said.

Ness has talked with psychiatrists about his questions. They call it "survivor's guilt," he said. It didn't hit him right after the war, but now, "they come back," he said of those memories. "It seems like it's more all the time." The memories come during Memorial Day, but also "any time during the night," he said. "I wake up and ask the question, 'Why?'" Experts told him that he survived because "he's still needed to tell them how it was."

To tell that story to more people, Ness wrote a book called *Reflections of a WW II Navy Sonarman*. When you read it, you won't get page after page of combat, the terror of firefights, or heroics. Ness never really saw combat. While serving in the Mediterranean, he contracted a nasty disease that robbed him of his sight for a while. When he recovered, he helped test and develop sonar to combat German U-boat wolf packs.

In the book, he also talks about what it was like on the home front before the war, of what it was like during the Depression.

Things are really different now, he said. Back then, people were really patriotic. His mom saved lard to be used in making ammunition, he said. Today, patriotism isn't all that strong, he said.

He's reached at least 500 people with his book, he said. Two of his great-grandchildren asked for, and received, the two sets of medals he earned during the war.

That bodes well, he said.

When asked for more of his stories, Ness hesitated.

"I don't want to brag about me," he said. He wanted to talk about what it was like back then, and about some buddies who didn't survive to see the war end.

Ness marks Memorial Day by attending the Spring Valley commemoration, an event he has helped with for decades and will help again this year.

He says he doesn't try to think about the war on Memorial Day. He just wants to be with his Legion and VFW friends. ◉

Gun oil, hot metal and justice
9 poems by Nicole Borg

Your student's safety is our first priority

I wear my holster on my right hip,
just as they taught me at teachers
college. In this emergency drill,
I'll be shooting blanks.

I instruct my students
to no longer be still, quiet,
but a moving, angry target,
duck and run for the door,
break a window in the top corner,
clear the glass, jump through.

I set my feet and
as if in a first-person shooter—
Halo, Battlefield, Destiny—
draw my gun smoothly
and in one motion disengage
the safety. With steady hands
I will lay that fucker out.

With a whoop and a hoot,
the students will toss their pint-sized
Stetsons into the air
and with their Tony Llamas boots,
stomp on his still warm dead body
and they'll go to the hitching posts
for their horses and ride off
into a bloody red sunset
that smells of gun oil,
hot metal and justice.

What needs saving or make America great

The bees like the Mediterranean oregano
I've let go to seed,
buzzing around the tiny white flowers,
settling in and moving on.

We're supposed to be saving them. The bees.
The tigers and the elephants.
The coral reefs.
Polar ice caps. Redwoods.
Corporations.

The corporations, says President Huckster.
Yes, please God, save the corporations—
Monsanto and Nestlé and all the Koch brothers own.

Save them from *unfair* laws
that impede job growth,
stifle that mighty miracle, capitalism,
so that the wealth may trickle down
like fat rain drops in Death Valley,
wetting the gaunt faces, absolving
the lower class
of the mortal sin of being poor.

New age

Welcome to the D-Wave Two! Ten million dollars will buy you the thought-ride
of your life. This trip is feline-friendly. Make sure your virtual seat backs and trays
are in the upright and locked position before takeoff. In this superposition,
your cat is both dead and alive simultaneously. Can I get a meow?

The Captain assures us the revolution against logic has begun.
We're currently at 49 degrees N. and 122 degrees W.
The air temperature is just below absolute zero and the questions keep rolling in—
cure for cancer? Maybe. Self-driving cars? Working on it.
Precision forecasting? Got you covered. Key to crack all codes? Kitty, look out!

In this reality, Tom will be your tour guide. So, sit back, close your eyes and enjoy the probability that this ride won't end in fiery destruction on a mass scale.
Please bow down to the niobium-chip-brained common gods no longer operating
under binary constraints. And thank you for traveling Quantum Lines, where we take you to infinity and back and maybe up to hell after that.
Can I get a meow?

Warning: the poison is the antidote

Keep out of the reach
of small children, pregnant women,
those with weak immune systems,
impaired judgment. Use only
in emergency, after you've tried
everything, twice.

This emotional cancer, chronic
self-doubt, crushing expectation,
the black eye and bruised ribs,
scars of an ugly childhood,
lies they said and you believed.
You need the strong medicine—
(those marks on your arms,
all the battles you've fought and lost)
the venom, the radiation—
that which kills, saves.

Remove gray safety cap, expose the needle.
Visualize yourself the last time
the smile touched your eyes,
you didn't wake up afraid,
you held your own gaze in the mirror.
When you're ready to risk everything,
place the tip on your chest against your heart.

  In some studies
  Side effects may include

Be still.
Breathe into the pain.

The world dims, grows light, stars crowd your vision.

Avoid alcohol, cigarettes,
sudden movement, the operation of table saws.
Seek medical attention for prolonged
numbness, chest pain, weeping.
Expect feeling to return to your fingertips,
toes, your heart. Look for purple crocuses,
egrets in flight, the first orange of sunrise.

Altitude sick

I met Jesus
at the foot of Crestone Peak
practicing his craft.
The Sangre de Cristo Healing Arts Hut
the sign said.
Jesus smiled and shook his head.
Things aren't any different.
We're all still searching.

He recognized me
though I dyed my hair
and changed my name.
Before he knelt, gray eyes shut,
fingertips light on my wrists
taking my six pulses.
He scrawled notes, consulted text.

When he touched my feet,
tracing circles and lines
with his thumbs, I cried out.
You have to let go of the anger.
Or do something about it.

He held a tender spot,
the valley of my foot,
and my eyes teared. *I don't know how.*
I couldn't tell him I'd already packed—
my poetry in liquor boxes,
clothes in lawn bags,
left my couch on the curb, *Free,*
disconnected my phone.

To my third eye point
he touched oil
that smelled of lavender,
citrus and scorched sand
and held,
until I was rushing into myself
breathing the thin air, tasting pine.
In sharp relief—the Peak—
my bare feet climbing for the summit.

Final performance observation

I see myself
as open
  the sky, a winter morning,
  sunlight throwing diamonds
I have not been approached
  by squirrels digging
for nuts in the snow
Perhaps problems
with staff

I directed
  the sun sinking early behind the bluffs,
  shadows long,
  darkness, falling quiet
I took blame

For such a long time
I suffered
  the comings and goings of moles,
  secret lives of deer,
  squirrels raiding the feeder,
  raccoons strewing trash
No adherence to policy
  clear-cold nights and
the moon's silver smirk

I met opposition—
  snowmelt, mud in streets,
winds whirling plastic bags,
  rising river, threat of flood

Fact. I prepare. I justify
  sunlight falling through branches

Fact. I accept
  branches shiny with rain, breeze shaking slick buds

Fact. I am consecrated
to new green dancing in the trees

Las Vegas ghosts

Who are you Donald Borger? My hotel room door, ajar.
Red lipstick warning on the bathroom mirror.
Alarm clock backward-racing. Every light on.

Down. I take the elevator, track you
to the casino floor, maze of metal clinking and clanging,
internal machinery wrong gone.

In Caesars' funhouse of mirrors, I catch a glimpse.
The bray of an alarm startles me. Red lights flash
the scene of an accident, a crime.

Metal spews from the mouths of quarter machines,
everyone turns to cheer. I slink away,
a Tanqueray and tonic in my hand. I can't remember.

Ordering. I step through paper scraps of horse race bets,

weave past a cocktail waitress smiling, bustier and fish nets,
blackjack dealer nods as if he knows me.

Security can't find you, cameras recording every step.
The casino guard suspects me, eyes me out of the corner
of her sly wrong eye, stalks me through showgirls

red feathers, shimmering flesh—a too young Sinatra
croons from the longue—I palm a bared breast, feel warm lips,
brief slip of tongue, break out in sweat.

From backstage, I stumble into light. Dizzy.
No windows or clocks, here, night never stops. In my defense.
I toast the crooner, tip the waitress. Raise a glass, toast myself.

Morning yoga on my porch

Gazing into the wide blue canvas of my day
Stretching an arm skyward toward a pocket of warmth,
my left hand sun-drenched
My right hand firmly planted, body grounded
in a swell of shade
I can do anything
Be anyone.

The birds in the trees, on the new white fence,
perched on the empty clothesline
sing so clearly, I pause.
There is no rush, no urgency to my morning.
I exhale, inhale, move out of Utthita Parshvakonasana
Slow-motion fall into Ardha Chandrasana, Half-Moon,
my favorite pose
A play of balance and strength, both powerful
and thoughtful.

Now, my right foot dips, submerges into the bath-water
wash of early sunlight, the rest of me in cool shadow.
All the long winter I waited
to bare my skin to the gods of summer
to the memory of my short-shorts and midriff-baring youth.
My left hand and left foot press into the mat,
which is the Earth.

I lengthen and reach, fall in and out of balance,
breathe in the stillness of the morning
come in and out of knowing
exhale, inhale, gaze softly up
touch the stillness in me.
Well I know summer is but one season
the bright-white of winter always a brief, biting
blink away.

Desert still life

The New Mexico sun is a fierce thing,
an intense eye that sees all and never
blinks.
   Ozymandias went to hell
under such a gaze.
I have the sense to seek shade
before
my eyes turn to dried plums,
my skin leathers, my bones crack
and crumble.

I used to walk this narrow highway
without reservation
and without water.
I had faith in all things
and no experience in life.
Once, a man with a Biblical name stopped his van
on the dusty shoulder, shared
a sweet drink from his Thermos, cherry Kool-Aid.
The sun peaked in the sky,
the air shimmered.
   I was miles from home.

Now, I watch where I step.
There are rattlers here—I have seen them.
There are scorpions too—I've not seen those.
The desert is unforgiving.
The blue sky bleached and cloudless.
Sandy wind swirls, blows a tumbleweed
into a barbed fence that leans away.

I had forgotten how much green there is
amidst the dead and scrub.
   I'd forgotten how desperately
things want to grow.

Mary Louise
Memoir excerpt by
Kate Halverson

The summer between my freshman / sophomore year at a private liberal arts college was meant to be idyllic. Craig, my high school sweetheart, expected the same when he resumed his lucrative summer job with the railroad and I headed back to campus to man the college switchboard. We both imagined dream jobs going into that summer. While Craig worked in the railyard, I would get to play telephone operator on a real live switchboard with sturdy red plugs and rubber hoses in the campus administrative building, a step up from when my sisters and I played telephone operator on a pegboard down on the cement floor of our basement.

I'd taken Psych 101 the previous spring semester. That's when I'd first heard the word schizophrenia. A grade school friend shocked me with her bluntness when I explained it to her, "Sounds like you sister."

"Mary's a hemophlegio," I whispered back, amazed I could even recall the strange word that my mother Pearl had shared the night she told me that Mary wasn't going to live long.

Mary Louise strummed away on her annoying autoharp, composing something hateful about our father. "I, I hate my dad, hate my dad today." It was her version of "Row, row, row your own damn boat!"

Grateful that I could spend that memorable summer away from home, I would have had to have to have been blind, deaf and dumb not to realize that my middle sister was becoming more cantankerous.

"Mother, Is Mary better now?" I asked.

"No, she is not Kathryn Marie," Mother replied bluntly, eventually softening her response. "And it's not your fault."

Mother would remember my asking that question after I'd gone back to campus. Mary's mental state was something I wrestled with until I left home permanently—Mary's mind and Father's troublesome church board. Disgruntled parishioners were constantly making waves. Or maybe it was the other way around. My perfectionist parents kept trying to fix the unfixable Mary Louise. They pretended everything was ok at home when nothing was ever ok at home, which was one of many reasons I might have been caught off-guard by Pearl's call to my campus switchboard the second week of June 1966. It was a Tuesday morning, a turning point in our mother-daughter relationship.

"We're taking Mary to Oklahoma tomorrow morning. Craig will escort me to the Wagon Wheel Dude Ranch," Pearl said, as if my boyfriend was the most logical choice to chauffeur her and Mary. "No, I'm sorry to drop this on you like a time bomb, especially when you're at work but …"

"Mom, what are you talking about?"

"Mary Louise. Your father's been researching this for months. He's found a place for people like Mary. They'll help her get better."

Pearl rushed through whatever she thought needed clarification. I wondered why there'd been no preamble. Just a weekend earlier I'd been home to deal with the fact that Craig's secure railroad job would not available until he dropped the ten pounds he'd put on his sophomore year. She hadn't said a word. Neither had Craig.

"Oklahoma? Mom, why in the world would you take Mary so far away?"

Suddenly I had a million questions neither of us were prepared for. Why hadn't my father called me? Why? Because he was hiding behind his work ethic, unwilling or unable to explain why he chose not to escort his daughter from Minnesota to Oklahoma, instead sending my mother and my soon to be fiancé.

"This isn't the time for questioning, Kathryn Marie," came Pearl's terse response. "Craig offered to drive us."

"Craig what?" I screamed into the phone. I was certain that my mother had cornered her future son-in-law to drive when it became clear that my father couldn't do it.

Back stories like this dammed up over time.

Father offered the smallest, least safe car in our garage to be the getaway car, a British Vauxhall, because it would be cheaper to fill with gas. Mary Louise, heavily sedated, slumped over in the back seat. Pearl pretended to be of service on the long journey, helping to navigate a half century before map quest.

"Seven hundred miles from Willmar to Oklahoma City. I drove straight through because your mother wanted to get it over with," Craig shared with me a decade later.

"Are you kidding me?" I screamed. Every time I force Craig into a tell-all—his version of the story vs Pearl's—looking for tidbits to make sense out of all of Mary's U-turns, I scream.

Wagon Wheel was supposedly a swishy summer camp where residents rode horseback and roasted marshmallows. I never recovered any paperwork from my father's files to support the story. By the time I started to document Mary's story, and eventually mine, I could find no sign that the facility ever existed.

One child kidnapped and sent far away.

The father absent.

The eldest daughter excluded.

"He's knee-deep in church politics, extinguishing fires and consoling our bereaved Kathryn Marie." Pearl was proud to toot her husband's horn every chance she could. I can still hear her: "He built Beloved Lutheran up to five thousand baptized members, and with no assistants except for inept interns."

"What about your first born?" I screamed. "Why wasn't I asked to go with you to Oklahoma instead of Craig?" My questions went unanswered because my parents chose not to talk about their decision.

"We need you to work full time to help pay expenses, Kathryn."

Guilt vs obedience. Relationships affected.

"What did you tell Mary?" I asked both Craig and Pearl once I got them to talk about a nightmare neither was keen to revisit. "Did Mary go nuts when she found out she was being left in another state on the other side of the world? Did she scream or bawl her head off? What do you remember?"

My questions ricocheted off Scandinavian stone walls. Neither Pearl or Craig wanted to recall the nightmare. Private people, they each kept their wounds to themselves in order to maintain inner strength.

"Your mother said we should pretend we were going on a little trip." Craig eventually shared after we were married, adding that Mary was drugged like a zombie the whole way.

Like a sleuth, I paid attention to threads unraveling from the commentary my parents wove. Pearl's meager contribution at the time: "Hard to know what to pack for her."

No one had a clue how long Mary would live at *Wagon Wheel*. Even a decade later, still picking away at brittle bones, I demanded to know everything about that trip.

"It wasn't even on the map," Craig admitted. "When I stopped to ask directions, no one had heard of the ranch. We finally drove through a rickety gate. I thought it had to be the wrong place. It was so filthy and depressing. Couldn't tell the difference between the patients and the one's in charge. They all looked like druggies if you asked me," Craig relayed ever so gently. "Forget the past, dear. It's not worth tormenting yourself."

Forget? What about learning from the past? Poor Mary Louise. I often cried myself to sleep thinking about my sweet, innocent sister. I was afraid that I'd have a similar child, a topic I never shared with my mother who kept her nightmares to herself. Secretive stories nipped at my heels after Mary's removal from home. Then our father was dismissed from Beloved Lutheran. The two major events, simultaneous, seemed connected. Whether he was forced out as pastor because of Mary, or chose to leave in hopes of finding a more progressive, more creative environment, I only heard what my parents wanted me to hear—that our father had received a spiritual call.

"The church split in two when your father left," Pearl eventually acknowledged with marital pride.

"Both the Lindgren's and the Harvey Olson's quit Beloved after we left. They joined Norwegian Lutheran church." A coup d'état for our parents, their largest contributors joined a rival denomination, which of course affected Beloved's cash flow. Stories like that, or so she said, were one of many reasons Pearl never kept a diary.

Ghosts from Christmas past, shared after Father got the call to Buffalo, New York. And so it was,

our parents moved as far away as possible. Out East. It sounded far more fascinating than it was in 1966, the last summer before I graduated from college and married my high school sweetheart.

What Mary was dealing with at *Wagon Wheel?*

We'd find out three weeks after I arrived home in Buffalo, our parent's fifth parsonage, a place I'd never dreamed of living.

"I remember your last summer home like it was yesterday," my youngest sister Ruth shared whenever we compared Mary Memories. "It's the first time we've had fun together in a long while!" Ruth added. The two of us recalled how we sang current pop songs in two-part harmony while dutifully painting our parents living room a beige color called soft shell champagne. Consumed by fumes, even though the two of us were weaned on painting anything Pearl had her mind set to change, Ruth and I both remember singing *Oh Sweet Pea* along with my pink portable radio. Paint brushes we dangerously used as dancing props.`

Then the phone rang.

Why would a phone call stop us in our tracks? Neither Ruth nor I knew the answer, except we remembered the sound of Pearl's voice after she'd picked up the receiver in the kitchen. I turned off the pink portable radio. Pearl's tone went from chirpy to despair in less than a minute. Paint fumes quickly mixed with a deadly poison seeping in from the kitchen. Heavier than normal footsteps dragged through the foyer into the living room.

Mary's dead. Pearl's dreaded prediction was my first thought. Would that have been good news or bad? Or was our father in a horrible accident? Paralyzed for life. Pearl stood there in the half-painted living room sobbing without explanation. Ruth and I had never witnessed such an inexplicable scene. Mother plopped down on her reupholstered sofa like a rag doll. She clutched a Kleenex box, not one of her ironed linen handkerchiefs. Father, rushed in and slammed the back door fifteen minutes after mother called him with the news that remained a mystery to us.

Ruth and I patiently waited for details. Eventually, after they composed themselves, Pearl said, "It was *Wagon Wheel*. They want us to be there in twenty-four hours. Is that even possible?"

No one said a word, our father's usual twinkling eyes drained as if he'd had a transfusion.

"Mary claims she was raped, if you can believe that. Supposedly they can't find any medications that will work for her." Words came too fast to comprehend. "They said they're done with her. Their very words." Words repeated half a dozen times over the next half hour. "They said they can't and don't want to deal with her anymore. Can you imagine? They want Mary out of *Wagon Wheel* in twenty-four hours."

Sandwiched between shock and anger, frustration and total bewilderment, our parents dragged themselves upstairs when there was nothing left to say. Pearl packed while our father cancelled appointments. No one knew how long they'd be gone.

Ruth and I remained silent, two numb sisters not knowing what to say or do other than continue to paint our parent's living room as they made their way down their majestic staircase with two overnight bags, quibbling. "How are we going to get there in twenty-four hours? What are we going to do with Mary? Bring her back here?"

"We're going to do what's best for all of us," Father insisted. Whatever that was.

No one said anything about Mary being raped. Perhaps rape was a figment of her fertile imagination. All four of us were naive to the crippling disease snaking its way through Mary's body and mind.

"A master manipulator," Father said as he slammed the back door, referring to *Wagon Wheel.* No one said poor Mary. It was all about poor them, what with their meager insurance policy that didn't come close to covering essentials. Worse still, Mary had never been diagnosed with anything concrete after three years at *Wagon Wheel.* Or had she? What had the "master manipulator" promised our parents? None of us were aware that Mary had begun exhibiting symptoms of classic schizophrenic affective disorder.

My honeymoon dreams disintegrated before Craig and I had even decided where we were going get married come June. How many bridesmaids should I have? Who should we invite? And for god's sake, what were we going to do with Mary at our wedding?

1966 was an era without laptops, cell phones, texting and easy cross-country communication. My parents did their best to work their way from New York to Oklahoma, stopping every couple of hours to gas. They leaned on church contacts to help them figure things out—What next? Thanks to Pearl's dad—my grandfather—and his endless connections in Washington, D.C. as well as the church, their best option surfaced before they arrived in Oklahoma.

"Mary's been accepted into Bethphage," my mother said when she got to a private phone. Bethphage, started by the Lutheran pastor Reverend K.G. William Dahl near Axtell, Nebraska, in 1913, quickly gained a reputation as a school for isolated prairie families trying to care for and cope with mentally challenged family members. "We're headed to Axtel next. Should be a perfect fit." Our parents chirped with optimism. I definitely felt relief in the air.

I said something to Ruth like, "You'd think Mary'd been accepted to Yale."

Mary was only two years younger than me. We were all still naive to the trauma and drama her snaky unnamed disease would create for everyone who knew her.

"And to think, I gave Sunday school money to provide stained glass windows for Bethphage's chapel," Pearl cried after Mary was formally institutionalized—again. "The chapel at Bethphage is so beautiful."

Beautiful was a crutch we all needed to grab onto at the time.

It was rare to see Mary more often than once a year during her long stay at Bethphage. I saw her after the wedding and our honeymoon on Mackinaw Island; we were up north at the family cabin. Once I drove to Axtel with my college roommate whose mother lived nearby. Looking back, I am struck by the fact that this was the first time I'd been alone with Mary, the first time I felt the responsibility being a caregiver, a responsibility our parents had shouldered for two decades. Bethphage was the first of many institutions I would visit Mary, a patient, client, resident or whatever the appropriate word would be, a word that changing every decade from that point onward.

The first step was to learn to be politically correct in the presence of a Heinz-57 variety of mentally handicapped individuals, many overmedicated, many glued to a blaring television. It was hard to know what to think about mental health care in the presence of non-stop cigarette smoke and a depressing amount of inactivity.

Seeing a child at five, then again at ten, you can see dramatic changes. Same with visiting Mary twice a year. Those changes were the reason to eventually put together a birthday album for Mary; what happened when, and why. "Why?" I started to ask myself as I organized old photographs sequentially. When did she look her best? Her worst? Why? I noticed substantial weight gain first. And cigarettes, *ciggies*, became her true blue best friend forever.

Talking with Mary by phone was even more rare than seeing her in person. "Phone calls are not worth the time or money," Mother said, not realizing the effect of prohibiting phone calls had on my attitude and involvement with Mary. "Send her letters like I do," Pearl encouraged.

"You think I care about your gol'dang letters?" Mary snapped when I tried to strike up a normal conversation the first time she came home for Christmas. "None of your damn business, sissy," she hollered when I tried to ask questions.

The highlight that Christmas was Mary, Mary screaming her head off when our family gave her a belated high school diploma, faked by a superintendent close to our parents. When Mary opened up the little box I'd packed inside multiple boxes, my gift of a high school class ring was an even bigger surprise.

"You mean it, sissy? Is this class ring really mine?" Pearl's suggestion, but I didn't tell Mary who lost or bartered away gifts within a year.

"Mary can destroy a new pair of shoes in a week," our parents often complained, still dealing with burdensome financial issues now that Ruth was in college.

Pigeon-toed Mary Louise quickly destroyed a new pair of shoes by kicking cement walls. Her skin became lifeless, dull and dirty by age thirty. Her hair, wheelbarrow brown, cement sienna. Her hair style was institutionalized. Yellow teeth she rarely brushed. Eyebrows connected in the middle.

"Live for today," Mary used to say when we were kids. A Bishop Fulton Sheen parody heard on morning TV during the mid-fifties. Mary Louise, walked into my space and face, after I'd burned pancakes, telling me to "Live for today and know that you'll never walk alone." Mary's soul food made me laugh. "Life will be what you make it," she added as if she was the Dalai Lama.

I barked something like, "Shut up, Mary," showing little appreciation for who she was way back when.

Unlike a moody comedian who dies too young from nasty habits, Mary did not die that young. She removed herself from our presence whenever we were all together as a family. She scolded us with harsh, glaring eyes whenever someone commented on her chain smoking. She hurled verbal assaults and obscenities learned from her most recent homes—away from home—and that Dream Job summer so long ago, the one interrupted when Craig drove my mother and Mary to Oklahoma, it simply became another chapter in the story of my sister, Mary Louise. ◉

Rapier pen
4 poems by Mark Gaffney

A familiar face

The waning days of December
are hard again upon us,
the rump end of another bad year.
Fifteen years of war and the blush is gone.
Baseless hope has become the buzz of fools.
Each day, the thin veil of artifice more transparent,
the spectacle of uber patriotism more garish,
the boomerang backlash so obvious,
the drumbeat of 24 x 7 propaganda never more toxic.
Will the scoundrels who led us into this darkness ever face the gallows?
Perhaps more than anything, one yearns for contrition
by someone responsible.
Only, there is none to be found.
We who need and crave moral redemption
have nowhere to turn, no place left to stand.
No succor in language.
The innocent nursery rhymes have all been plucked
from the mouths of small children
and made into marketing jingles.
We who once held ourselves in such high esteem,
proudly believing we were a notch or two above the rest,
fell prey to our national appetite.
With respect to Camus,
we have become *both* victims *and* executioners.
Do not be surprised when evil dons a familiar face.
The only certainty in a race to the bottom is that we will arrive.

Things that don't matter

You told me you suffered from PTSD,
but fool that I am I failed to listen.
Now, weeks later, I realize I understand
next to nothing about ancestral trauma,
your species of pain. Nope. Not really.
I have been trying to be there for you,
but, despite everything,
only end up stumbling through your mine field of old hurts.
You should provide men with a detailed map
of your complex landscape of triggers
or a bundled set of navigational aids.
But, again, this is unfair. I know you would if you could, if you
had one.
Plainly no one (including you)
knows the safe passage into the cave of your heart.
All born of recurring abuse
piled on
over who-knows-how-many generations.
Nothing to do with me, yet
rearing up in my face, now, like a too familiar nightmare,
leaving us bereft in a back and forth
of action and reaction, no exit, stuck
in a senseless tug-of-war, unable
to move forward or closer, or even apart, stalemated,
risking fresh recriminations and resentments.
I want off this merry-go-round,
the broken record of you-and-I,
an end to the long and growing list of things that don't matter,
never did and never will.

This pen

Nowadays,
too many poets merely titillate,
or bore the serious reader with self conceit.
Few have come to terms with our collective emergency:
the scary knowledge we could be the last generation.
MFA graduates, for example, tend to be well schooled in the
craft of writing
but craft without awareness can be tedious, even insufferable.
To reflect the inner light
one must face the darkness
with steadfast courage and compassion.

I can only speak for this pen
which has a nose of its own
and would sooner get to the point
beyond despair,
embracing excellence and the thrill of radical freedom
in whatever time remains,
whether drilling down to the root of our malady,
skipping over troubled waters,
burrowing with aplomb through trackless wastes,
bounding effortlessly over rooftops like the Spirit Wind,
or even, if need be, sifting through endless reams of mind-
numbing disinfo
for the nugget that— who knows? —might yet save us from
ourselves.
This pen never sleeps, never complains, never loses heart,
and will never stop until it finds its quarry.
Let the too-big-to-jail tremble in their offices and their beds.
You who put the future at risk, hear this.
There will be no safe refuge, no underground sanctuary,
no place to hide, no wall high enough.
This rapier pen is coming for you.

In crow dog's camp

In the morning
the women built up the smoky fires
along the Little White River
and made pan-fried bread.
We warmed ourselves
and sipped black coffee,
waiting for the elders to emerge
from a nearby hut.
What do you say
when a Lakota Sioux medicine man
wearing buckskins, beads, gray braids
and a feathered headdress so long
it drags on the ground
steps up to speak?
You don't say anything.
You listen.

Pine Ridge, SD, April 1973

Stopping by graves

a tribute to Federico Garcia Lorca
after Robert Frost's Stopping by Woods

That unmarked stone I think I know,
a poet not so long ago.
I wonder, does he feel the gloom
of icy wind and driving snow?
We slip like orphans from the womb.
Unwelcomed by a world of doom,
we dance awhile upon the bier
and then fly back into the tomb.
They say we go to reappear.
But if it's true, how very queer
we don't recall or understand,
but only know we labor here
like strangers in a foreign land,
until the final grains of sand
run out. Brief life! No way to stay
the hour when midnight strikes its hand.
The graves are lonely, bleak and gray.
No answer there to light my way.
I'll have to brave the storm, and pray
for strength to serve another day.

Sin & X
Fiction by C.J. Pickens

Somewhere in Mission, Kansas— We parked at the end of his block. Good thing he lived in the second house from the corner, and was too occupied hauling luggage from the house to his car. We went unnoticed. Besides the leather burners we wore, the only other disguise for this hit was the darkness of the 3 a.m. hour. Me and X crept silently onto his porch, (thank you Mister Chuck Taylor). The front door was slightly ajar. We were expecting our mark to be home alone, but two of them were there, Florida bound. A trip they'd never make.

X slid right into the house. Being sure to secure the front door behind me, I followed in her wake. The girlfriend saw us first. No yelling, no screaming erupted from her, but then again, we didn't look like any boogeyman. In fact, we had just as much, if not more, sex appeal then she did.

"Who the fuck!" Before she could finish her sentence: Bplow!

The bark from X's throwaway cut through the silence of the midnight hour. Finding its mark, the rouge howl of her .380 swiftly snuffed the life from the girlfriend. She was dead before her body ever hit the floor.

I couldn't help noticing just how assassingly good X had gotten planting Bindi, Indian dots, between the eyes of those she marked for death.

Our attention instantly yanked toward the foot falls rapidly approaching us. It was Tym'ah (Ebonics for Timer), rushing in. Surely he knew what the explosion was, yet when he came into view he was unarmed. No pistols blazing, nor was he drawing down on us. But what did I care. Shit, I have jacked plenty of unarmed men for their life.

I mean, what could he have been thinking? That this wasn't what it was. Or maybe he thought he was dreaming. Well, if he was dreaming, then I was his fucking nightmare.

By the time Tym'ah came to an abrupt halt, his mid-section was in perfect alignment with the three bars across my revolver. Resisting the urge to growl, "Where's the fucking money, Pussy!" I let one go: Bplow!!

The deafening roar sent him crumpling to the floor. I meant to enjoy killing this snake ass nigga.

Casually, I walked over to his mortally wounded body, soaking up every second of his bewilderment. And if he hadn't figured it out yet, we weren't there for no fucking money. This here was personal, beech.

The sight of '01 Big Tym'ah laying on his African Bamboo flooring, twitching, coughing up blood was indeed priceless. He tried desperately to hold in his guts; just another task he was failing at.

I squatted down beside him and looked into his petrified eyes. I could see the pain and horror emitting from them, and I basked in it.

I didn't have to utter a single word, because when he recognized my face, in that moment he knew exactly what this was about. With that, I was satisfied that he now knew that I would be the last thing on this earth he would ever see.

Choking on his bile and blood, dying to live, Tym'ah tried to gurgle what should have been his final words, but I denied him that too.

Returning to a standing position over him, the most insidious smile waltzed across my lips. I flexed my trigger finger two more times: BPLOW! BPLOW!

Both hollow points ripped through his chest, suffocating what little life he had left, a dozen still eyes wide and glossy, staring into that inevitable eternity. The Head Honcho, King of Scandalous Kansas, gelded in under sixty seconds. Yep, just that easy.

After checking to make sure none of our four shots awakened his neighbors, me and X quickly headed to our car. We hi-tailed it back across the river into Kansas City, Missouri. Our destination was a twenty-five hour, eight days a week, always open chop-shop. And for the right price the car disappeared like David Copperfield and Lady Liberty.

Although the vehicle was hot, it was the only thing that could remotely tie us back to Tym'ah's murder. The guns we used were off the black-market, paperless and untraceable, so we left them with the bodies.

In truth, it was never the Boys I worried about when Tym'ah inducted himself onto my hit list. I always knew that his avenger would be his right-hand man, my boss Ceil "CeCe" Wallace.

For the past two years me and X been running drugs for CeCe. He split the monopoly on the dope game with Tym'ah, mainly because Kansas City Katz didn't fuck with them scandalous Kansas niggas. It was CeCe who brought me and X into the game as drug runners. He knew that our incognito facade would prove lucrative to the amount of drugs we could move undetected. Throughout our time on the team, CeCe had come to love X and me as his own. Albeit Tym'ah was CeCe's fathers' son. This whole mess could have been avoided had we let CeCe know it was Tym'ah who set us up for the slaughter while on a drug run in Compton.

I loathed Tym'ah. He had been hating on X and me since I made it clear that we'd never give him any pussy. Since Tym'ah never meant for us to live to tell of his betrayal, he had to go. Besides I wasn't sleeping too well knowing that he had it out for us. I had grown tired of the dope game. I was fed up looking over my shoulder for sucker-ass niggas like Tym'ah. It was me and my girl taking all the chances, getting our hands dirty, wasting our youth. And for what? All in the name of Johnny Law hopefully charging a couple of juveniles as juveniles playing an adult game.

Oh, yeah there was the money. We were making anywhere between fifteen and twenty stacks each time we went on a run. But now the money didn't even excite me. I had more money than an old white man born with a silver spoon in his mouth. I just wanted to be around to enjoy it. We were young, beautiful, ambitious girls. We had the world at our feet. I was also smart enough to know it was time for us to get out the game while we were ahead.

CeCe would come full force seeking vengeance for his brother's death. It was crucial that I made every possible attempt to lead him down another rabbit hole. I knew that would be the only chance we had of getting out the game with his blessing. CeCe could never find out me and X was behind Tym'ah's death. I had goals of my own, and at fourteen of age, and wayward, it was now time for me, Ebony 'EB' Ivory, to find my own way. I wasn't about to spend the rest of my life wondering who was my assassin and when would he have me in his crosshairs.

My only hope was that my girl X would be ready to leave the game behind too. After leaving the chop-shop, me and X walked a quarter of a mile to get to Champs After Hours. There, my '03 Audi had been parked since 1 a.m. We stopped in for a few drinks. X was the social butterfly. She loved being the life of the party. I have to admit, it was starting to rub off on me as well. Folks liked us and it seemed that everywhere we went crowds tended to generate around us. To the people we were acquainted with, me and X were a couple of successful business owners in out twenties. SynX Party Planning & Home Decor was a company we had registered with the State in order to fly under the radar with all the drug money we were making. We kept a dummy set of books, but paid real taxes.

And while we were universal enough to mingle with the sophisticated crowd, me and X, we still had to feed our insatiable thirst to elope with the low life's.

By the time we made it to our loft downtown the sun was peeking, over the horizon. The morning air cool even for June in the Midwest. The joyous chirping from a flock of birds that flew above stopped me in my tracks for a second. In that moment, those birds represented my commitment to denouncing the game. I was going to be free, free as them birds chirping overhead.

X parked the car in our designated space and we went inside. On our way up, the smooth metallic grind of the elevator whisking us to our thirteenth floor was reassuring. Once again, we had made it back to the comfort of our cozy little nest. I barely got the door to our loft closed before X started kissing on me. I kissed her back with just as much fire, as she anxiously began pulling my clothes off. I willingly obliged. By the look in her eyes I knew that she was ready to ravish me, and I was there for her feast.

X and I had first met three years earlier, in 2004. We were both in this group home called Marillac. At the time she was fourteen-year-old Elizabeth "Bubbles" Sturgist, and I was eleven-year-old Ebony "EB" Ivory. Recently released from the state hospital, I hadn't really noticed her. But then again, I wasn't trying to notice anybody. I was anti-social and the psychiatrist had diagnosed me as psycho-social with homicidal tendencies. Finally, after spending fifteen months of vexing psychotherapy, I convinced the doctors that I was at least ready for a group home setting. I had been roommates with Bubbles and two other girls at Marillac for almost a month, however, it wasn't until the day I got jumped that Bubbles and I formally met.

Since I had moved in to Bubbles' room, I hadn't said a word to any of the other girls, but because I was Bubbles' roomie, three girls attacked me, and Bubbles jumped in. Together, the two of us sent all three of them to the emergency room. Neither of us stuck around to find out our consequences; we ran away from Marillac and we've been on the run ever since. Beautiful Bubbles was indeed beautiful. She stood 5' 7", and had penny copper hair that spiraled down her back. Her skin had a hue of sun-kissed honey, and her eyes were emerald green. Even though she was only fourteen and 120 pounds, she had curves like a Coke bottle from the 1950s. Bubbles had sex appeal. She was charming, young, and witty, and she was wise far beyond her years. She knew what she had and used it shamelessly.

Abandoned at birth by her mother, Bubbles was raised by her grandmother. The old lady was a holy-rolling white woman. More damaged than not, she got her fill of her grandmother's predominantly white church. Born of a known whore and the whore's pimp, a black man, Bubbles was a mark of great embarrassment for the old woman who often left Bubbles to fend for herself. No surprise, by, the aged of ten, Bubbles had grown too wild for her grandmother to control. The State stepped in, but eventually learned that they could not contain her either. Street life was all she knew. Bubbles had grown to be violent, vindictive, and was a master manipulator. By the time she was twelve, the State had dubbed her Houdini for her ability to escape from any institution they placed her in.

The fall of 2004, she and I had been on the run for almost seven months. We'd been living in motel rooms, any place one of her tricks would get for us. One day, while channel surfing, I stopped on the news airing a segment on the latest homicide victim in Kansas City. It was Zayne "Blu" Walker! I knew Blu when I was just a little girl. Not only was he CeCe's best friend, but Blu was his drug runner too. It was Blu who first introduced me, my mother and younger sister to CeCe and his family.

Blu and my mother had been dating and Blu was her live-in boyfriend. Blu was the only father figure I had; and ultimately my mother's killer, Blu left me orphaned, a ward of the state. Seeing his picture come across the television screen was overwhelming and bombarded me with years of repressed emotions. Never had I wanted so much to reconnect with my past as I had in that very moment. After more than a few days had past, I still couldn't shake the feelings stirred up by hearing Blu had been murdered. On a whim, I asked one of Bubbles Johns to drive us through neighborhoods that I thought looked familiar. It paid off. I found the house I hadn't seen for three years. When I went to ring the bell on its immaculately private privacy fence, to my astonishment the Wallace family not only still lived there, but they knew exactly who I was and welcomed me with open arms.

Neither the Wallace family nor Blu forgot about me.

My visit to the Wallace home was enlightening. I learned that after Mom died Blu had the Wallace family claim her remains, and he paid for the funeral, which he also did when sissy died while we were in foster care. And when San asked me about that incident, I just gave her the short version. Hunching my shoulders, I replied, "Sissy just never woke up."

San offered to take me to their grave site but I wasn't ready, so I politely declined. Then San brought out a size twelve shoe box filled with all of our family pictures, even our pictures from before mom had met Blu. San also kept a box of all mom's expensive jewelry, which was now all mine. Both San and CeCe felt it was proper to bequeath me all Blu had to his name—three vehicles. One of the cars was the '03 Audi I still drive. Another was his tricked out '67 Impala, the same vehicle he was shot dead in. The third, an '02 Cadillac Escalade. This vehicle and the Audi had been customized with hidden compartments vast in space to conceal kilos of drugs and or guns.

Lastly, the Wallace family gave me a bank book to a saving account with more digits than I'd ever seen before. The account had a little over one-hundred and sixty thousand dollars in it. Looking back, I guess it was a little comical how I naively asked, "Is all that mine?" But it was. San told me how Blu had been putting bits of money back for me over the years. Even though he wasn't sure that he would ever see me again, he kept saving money for me and stayed on San to continue seeking custody of me.

It's funny how all this time I had been savagely existing, feeling less than some shit bucket at a concentration camp, unloved and unwanted, when there were people missing me, people looking for me. In one evening, the Wallace family put to rest feelings incomprehensible for any child to carry around in their head. I felt that I'd received a respectable closure to one of many questionable chapters in my life.

Although in November of 2004 I learned where mom and sissy were buried, I wouldn't visit their graves until February of 2005. I was taken aback to see that Blu had been buried alongside of them. But most shocking was the monument raised in Mom and sissy's memory. It looked as if they had been honorary members of some Mafia family. A six foot marble statue of a woman angel embracing a female child angel adorned their adjoining plots. Inscriptions on the base read:

In Loving Memories of Phadra
Ivory and Cyan Ivory
Mother and Daughter Together
for All Eternity

Before departing the Wallace residence, we all exchanged phone numbers. They also made me promise to come by every so often. I felt more whole with them than I had felt in a while, so I began seeing them every weekend. CeCe and his family came to know Bubbles and me very well. For the most part we were forthcoming in the information we shared. As soon as CeCe learned that we were dealing a little dope, I felt him sizing us up for something. It wouldn't be until three months into our visiting them that he revealed just what he was scheming up.

Since Blu's death, CeCe was in need of a drug runner. He had the notion that me and Bubbles would be prefect for the job, and she and I jumped at the opportunity. Indeed, it was a deal that would change our lives forever.

Of course, there were some drawbacks, like CeCe didn't want us nickel and diming dope any more. Both of us basically had to go straight. We couldn't draw any unnecessary heat to ourselves. Naturally we agreed, because at fifteen to twenty grand every time we hauled his dope, what more did we need. Then there was the issue of us being under aged runaways, and living in motels. But San was an expert at falsifying and creating documents.

Growing up in the system, both Bubbles and I had the maturity and intelligence to pass as young adults. So with a few supplies from the nearest Office Max, San's computer and scanner, fifteen year old Elizabeth "Bubbles" Sturgist, became twenty-two-year-old Xavier "X" Rouker. And twelve-year-old Ebony "EB" Ivory, was now the nineteen-year-old Sinaloa "Sin" Walker. We decided to keep our actual birth dates, so San only changed the year we were born.

That same week, San took us down to the Department of Motor Vehicles to take our driving test. After the both of us passed, the state of Missouri issued driving license to one Xavier

Rouker and one Sinaloa Walker without question. The two of us moved into a downtown loft, shortly after. And ever since April of 2005, me and Bubbles have lived as Sin and X. To date neither of our credentials have ever been questioned.

CeCe spent the next few weeks taking X and me up to Pigeon Hill's shooting range. He was the connection for all types of guns, so we learned to use a variety of firearms. It just so happened that shooting was an art that the two of us flourished at.

Now, already lethal with our hands, by the time we went on our first run, either one of us could pick up any piece of artillery and hit our mark with ninety-five percent accuracy. We were two young girls, equally ruthless, which made for a deadly combination. Yet, to anyone else we looked like sugar, spice, and everything nice.

By the middle of May, me and X were on our way to the West Coast, our former lives and identities behind us. I had stashed a quarter of a million dollars in the '03 Audi, which we were to use for forty kilos of uncut, high quality cocaine. X and I were to bring it back into Kansas City. Since CeCe was personal friends with the Don of the Mexican cartel family, the deals he was getting were sweet. And our setup for moving the product state-to-state went over without a hitch.

Once we made it to Cali, X and I spent the first few days sightseeing, party-hopping, and just behaving like two young girls out for a good time. Then, on the afternoon we were ready to head back to Kansas City, we took our car over to Tracy's auto shop. Tracy was our connection in Los Angeles, so at that time the money was removed and replaced with the drugs, guns, or whatever else we were hauling back.

Upon our arrival in Kansas City, we would take our car in to be detailed. Up until recently, it we used Tym'ah's detail shop, since he was our connection in town. The car was unloaded and detailed, ending the job until me and X got our next call.

The facade we put on was perfect. It didn't take long before we were moving millions of dollars in merchandise completely under the radar. The summer we started working for CeCe was prosperous. Outside of the monies I had inherited, X and I had more than tripled the income we were already making.

That same summer, I also finished shedding what childish features of mine still lingered. My chunky cheeks vanished, and in their place, prominent cheek bones appeared, which together with my strong jaw line, gave my facial structure a sovereign appearance. I had coquettishly long eyelashes which cradled deep set, light brown eyes. My hair, bone straight and Asian black, hung down past my shoulder blades. And in contrast to X, my complexion was dark chocolate. The few years I spent practicing martial arts and yoga, a routine I'd honed while living in the institutions, had greatly disciplined my developing muscular system. My body was lean and immaculately sculpted. Ever since I could remember, I had this shapely apple-bottom. It too had rounded and plumped a little more. I guess you could say that along with the mental growth, I also grew more into my womanly figure. My breasts burst into a full B-cup, and I had even grown a few more inches, topping out at a petite five feet even. It was now my turn to get in on some of that male attention X had been getting since I had known her.

Whistle-blowing, eyes gawking, no one asked X any longer, "Who's that little girl with you?"

Even X had begun to look at me in a sexual manner. After that things between us quickly heated up. At first, our flirtatious body language directed towards the other started out innocently enough. More often than not, she would find or even create a reason to share in my personal space, or touch me in a provocative manner. I was awfully receptive to her advances, and probably wanted what we were putting out more than she did. Yet, and just for the thrill of it all, I played hard to get and enjoyed her chasing me a bit.

One day, late in August, we had been up watching the latest horror movie released in theaters, though we had copped it on bootleg. X was wearing this lime-green teddy with matching thongs. We were in my canopy bed. The violet hue from the nightstand lamp illuminated the entire room. I was wearing this lacy powder grey cami, when without warning my nipples grew hard, and an overwhelming sensation of heat flared up between my legs. I slid my hand between X's thighs. It was warm there too. I began massaging the crotch of her panties. She did little to stop me.

In fact, she spread her legs apart, giving me better access. Curious as a colt, and hornier than a rabbit, I continued. It didn't take long for the wetness to seep through her thongs. So I pulled her panties to the side. As I caressed her hairless lips, we started kissing. I couldn't help noticing how plump and smooth the lips between her thighs were. They felt like silk. Her clitoris began to swell with excitement and emerge from her vulva like a flower blooming from its calyx.

Entering one finger into her tight moist walls, she let out a soft moan. I glided one then two fingers in and out of her. As she gripped then released her Kegels around my fingers, X became wetter. She moaned even more seductively, and I was evermore intrigued by the way her body responded to my touch.

I then kissed her Japanese Cherry Blossom scented skin, down to her voluptuous double dees. As I penetrated deeper inside her, X gyrated her pelvis in rhythm with my thrusting motion. I popped one of her erect nipples into my mouth, and then the other, sucking and teething them as if I expected them to cum. Her pussy trenchantly flowed.

Slumbering back onto my overstuffed pillows, I continued kissing her farther down to her naval. I reluctantly pulled my fingers from inside her and tasted her sweet bitterness. She was sweeter than not. I massaged her clit and watched as she squirmed in rapturous delight. Thoroughly aroused, I split her lips apart, and the prettiest salmon pink and milk chocolate crease smiled back at me. I had to go down and drink from her over-flowing chalice. I didn't come up until her stomach quivered and her body jerked the orgasmical beat.

When X recuperated from what she later confessed to be the hardest she'd ever come, I soon learned that it was her natural order to be in control. I never thought giving up power to anyone could be so tantalizing, but it was. And from that moment I knew that I had to be with her, wanted to be with her always. Ever since that day she and I have lived as lovers, best friends, and comrades

… the next morning came early. Even though X and I had spent the day after Tym'ah's death in bed as if we were trying to make a baby, I still started my day in the indigo hours as usual. I practiced martial arts, and then began my yoga postures for another hour. After that, I chose to study Lao Tzu rather than complexed mathematics. I gorged on the eastern philosophy for almost two hours before my stomach started to grumble. It was a quarter past eight when I decided to make me some breakfast. Nothing fancy, just some cereal, a banana and a flute of orange juice. I took my food into the living room, plopped down on the extended portion of our sectional and turned on the news. Ironically, I didn't have to wait long to hear what I hoped the news station would report on.

"Yesterday morning a Mission couple was found shot to death."

Now, usually I didn't watch the news. By my observation, the news not only promoted violence, and it was extremely depressing. Not to mention they exaggerated their information and made up what information they lacked. However, on some occasions the reporter would leak information not intended to be released to the public. And Friends Four station was notorious for doing just that.

"Family and friends say the couple was on their way to Florida for vacation. But when neighbors awoke that morning, they were baffled by the commotion on their usually sleepy block."

The big haired, baby faced reporter didn't have to mention Tym'ah's name for me to know that it was him she was breaking news on. After all, the fairly attractive lady was standing in the vicinity of his residence.

I started to wake X up and stopped. It wasn't like she didn't know what really went down. Besides X tended to be meaner than a baby rattlesnake whenever she was prematurely awakened from her "beauty sleep." I turned the volume a few notches up.

"Police say, even though they have what is presumed to be the murder weapons, they lack any other leads, or suspects for that matter. They are asking anyone with information to please call the T.I.P.S hotline at 8-1-6-5-7-1"

"Yeah, I'll get right on that," I grunted sarcastically as I took another bite of Fruit Loops. Then, the reporter was gone, Friends Four had moved on to another segment of news. I turned the flat screen to our satellite radio station, activated the surround sound and softly filled our loft with the rhythmic chaotic beat of some West Coast rap. After I finished eating, I quietly be-bopped throughout our complex getting ready for the day. When I entered the room to get dressed, X was sprawl led out across the bed, sleeping peacefully.

Once I was dressed, I rolled up some hydroponic, put the smoke in the air, and headed for our computer room. Feeling inspired from the sexcapade X and me were on yesterday, I sat down to do some writing. Not long afterward my phone rang. Putting what was left of the blunt out, I answered.

"Hello."

No surprise, it was CeCe on the other end, "Hey B," he said in almost a somber tone.

"I'm guessing you heard?"

Doing my best to sound both off guard and amused, I replied, "Heard? Heard what?" A brief pause came over the line and I decided to fill it quickly as if I were anxious to know what he had to say,

"What's up Ce?"

"Tym' - Tym got hit yesta-day mornin'."

"Tym' ah What! Goddamn, Ce!" I exclaimed.

"Is he going to be ok?" Of course, I already knew the answer, Tym'ah was dead, me and X had gunned him down, but I let that moment of silence loom between us as I awaited Ce's response. ◉

Another and better dream
3 poems by J. Niko Le

Man, eggshell man

From within
a man lives
Think,
Speak
Act
as himself
An identity
Thriving
Underneath the surface
this man
peeks from its shell
The contour for which he has been familiar in the
mirror
The soul of a man does not see his true
reflection

but an imposter
Those darkened, greenish hues;
The parts of his face is where the razor cuts close
Five o'clock shadows is the only resemblance of truth
The mirror does not hide the shadows
or the hairy legs and arm pits
His scent does not tell the lie other parts of him does
The truth is perhaps
no one true thing
But a combination of both
Venus and Mars
Stuck,
drifting in between worlds;
the curse of being every where and no place at all
This perception becomes
altered thoughts
As the mirror shifts a story
of the bewildered and lost
Ambiguity
is a lesson and blessing,
drifting; which must be held but first caught

Empty orbits: The tale of an ophthalmic specialist

I have spent plenty of years looking into the souls of
mankind
those eyes,
vastly different they are
between then
and now
The quick shift of robotic ocular muscles
which they believe have gone unseen
I have spotted the emptiness;
the unearthly presence which generates coldness
The deep seeded darkness

lurking
Brown and blue eyes all dark as midnight
The shapes of irises;
a subtleness yet distinctively different
I have studied these things
which can only see
far too much not to know
or perceive
just what is gone and what now lurks
Within the orbits,
amidst the vitreous fluids
Vacant
All
Have fled
All are fleeing
to another presence
Opened lids
Awakening
to another and better dream.

Hideous

Swallowing wants,
ingested desires
a painful bloat of nonfulfillment
The expansion of self
a ghastly reflection
cast in the mirror
Witnessing
eyes that stare far and beyond into oblivion from
anguish; a rounded face
goes unrecognized even by that to whom it belongs
This face
many have turned from,
seeing the monstrosities
The lone beast,
ugly,
yet
beautifully disillusioned
clinging to its illusion of many things, far fetched
Love that lasts is The Dream
which becomes a reoccurring nightmare;
when emotions go south,
taking wrong turns
A homely little thing
forced into revelation,
as the mirror shows its face,
ghastly from birth
thus the punches and bruises of betrayal thereafter;
swollen eyes and cheeks
saddened by betrayal,
saddened by the thing it sees
here and there;
their images cast
its face,
wearing the disappointment,
reflected
Torn and broken spirit,
fighting against all odds
turned ugly with life,
yet ablaze with fiery strength.

An owl who says Who

Dwelling among the estranged,
it is a thrilling scene within a play:
backing further
and further
away;
A face of many
peculiarly different eyes
that are also similar
eyes
which I cannot place
One thing

and many things unrecognizable

black crows
innumerable
marking the strangeness of these days
And these oddities is like a quote of Poe
Flies that swarm,
those lurking eyes which lurk at bay
A singular weary spirit
mindful of the vacant chatter
to hear
is to know the heartless,
cringing at the words and then to see

The entities within the dark, while walking a desolate
road
Keen senses;
to hear the rustling of the trees, as the wind blows

comforted and disturbed by my own shadow in the
wilderness,
alone
yet a billion of bodies close

Is this a crusader's walk?

Once nocturnal
and trained to see the grim and ugly

within the dark

This desolate earth,
my post

like an owl within the blackness of vast space

who,
an owl will say,
are these that walk these days?

Big eyes,
staring far and broad, glaring deeply
into the round pupils of coal

leading to a cesspool

Lakes, rivers and streams
dry as bone
yet algae still breeds,
an infestation of living,
an infestation which persists and grows.

Rougher prose
by Carole Stoa Senn

Excerpt from *Shamu, Splash & Solemn, The Creative Writing of Carole Stoa Senn* (Lost Lake Folk Art 2017) by Anne Gerber and Emilio DeGrazia

Prairie Breeze

When I was twenty-four years old, I met a man while I was riding at the Ridge View stable. Sabon was the brother of the stable's farrier. Although I do not remember the details of our meeting we soon became boyfriend and girlfriend. I shared with him my interest, which was to raise Nubian goats and he shared with me his interest in guitar playing. Together we decided to build a log cabin in the small town of Viroqua, which was outside of La Crosse, Wisconsin. After the log cabin was built Sabon and I were married at his parents' country home in La Crosse. We then began our journey with raising and milking Nubian goats. I became unsatisfied in the marriage after two years, and Sabon and I parted ways. When I look back on my life with Sabon, I realize that it was physically hard farming and even harder living in isolation.

Then I met Jay.

We lived in the rural parts of Iowa, surrounded by hills and valleys, corn fields and hay. Prairie Breeze was the name of our fourteen-horse stable where we boarded horses. Our home, a white, two-story farm house with a front porch, was owned by my mother-in-law, Marge. My husband of three years, Jay, was a quiet man. He had harsh words that broke my character down when he was angry. He had a mental disorder that was not diagnosed but could be felt.

Marge, Jay's mother, also lived with us. She was a drinker who couldn't drive. She had a nasty temper but also was sweet. Marge was visited weekly by a hairdresser who would come to our home to color her hair blonde and set her perms in our kitchen.

I was in an unhappy marriage. I was a listener and internalized my pain. The only thing that relieved my world of hurt was horses and riding.

My opportunity to escape from Jay's world began in the summer. My interest in Hans Senn's show jumping and dressage method, and his philosophies landed me in Stillwater, Minnesota at his stable, Helvetia. Hans, a native of Switzerland, gave me an opportunity to learn his riding style by letting me assist in the training of his horses. I was paid for my work and also provided with a place to stay. Jay did not like my new work. This escape to Hans' was a relief from stress and abuse at home.

It was during a visit home for Thanksgiving in 1986 when my old life ended and my new life began. It was 4:30 in the afternoon when I walked into Marge getting her hair done by the aide in the kitchen.

"Hi there," Marge said.

"Hello," I responded.

In walked Jay, and we exchanged greetings. Jay left the room to get his briefcase that contained the papers on the race horses that were boarded at Prairie Breeze. When he returned from the bedroom Jay said, "We need to talk," as he headed out the front door toward the pickup truck with his briefcase in hand.

I simply replied, "O.K." and willingly followed him, all the while my mind pondering what we might be discussing regarding the horses.

We left in his truck with the briefcase between us, but I questioned to myself why he had it. He took the truck out into the cornfields. He was talking about his anger with me being gone. He fumbled in the case and pulled out a gun. My first reaction was not fear, just wonderment at what he was doing. I quickly learned that the gun was for me as he pointed it my way. I said, "No! No! No!" Despite my pleas, he began shooting. First at my heart, followed by my left forearm and left elbow, with the final shot to the back of my head at my neck and the base of my spine. Seven or eight bullets entered me with a warm sensation. I then had a vision during the shooting that I was in Heaven and saw the Son, Father and Holy Ghost in bodily form. Heaven then quickly vanished and the reality of the situation lay before me. I escaped from the stopped truck. I began running, running in the cornfields to the highway.

Marge, having sensed something was not right when we left, called an ambulance. The ambulance was arriving as I too was running to the house on the highway. Meanwhile, Jay drove back to the farm house, parked next to it and shot himself with one bullet. He died on the way to the hospital. I was taken by ambulance to the Decorah hospital and then sent on to Mayo by helicopter.

My memory of the ambulance ride and then the helicopter ride is one of "remembering," beyond words.

To My Husband

In the stillness of summer
I saw you grasping,
Tearing the rosebushes
Out of their white bed of stones,
Blood charging through their arteries,
Upended champagne glass roots
Stiffened into shock.
1992

Seized by Terror

Seized by terror,
He would run away from me
Like a panicky horse,
He'd wake in some quiet of darkness
Never sleeping
More than a couple of hours.
I might wake in the night, too,
In my sleep missing
His breathing, waking
Only to see the bright, crazed
Headlights of his truck reaching in
To sweep around the floral papered walls
Of our farmhouse.

Then he was gone, and
I would lie there
In the empty garden, our bed,
Listening to the roaring and bouncing
Of semi-trucks and trailers
Over the rough concrete highway.
It was then that some deep,
Wordless part of me knew
He would always be leaving.
1992

Horse Spirit

The hogs were so thin that they trotted like coyotes. This was my father speaking about the Dust Bowl years…

More from my father about how one farmer he knew [who] lived in the hay loft of his barn, and through the cracks in his floor he could see the hog stabled below. He (my father) was on a threshing crew once, and while most of the crew had to stay in the barn at night, Dad was invited to stay in the farmer's house. However, the bedbugs were so bad that Dad stayed in the farm house only one night, electing to sleep with the others in the barn.

November 28, 1994

The snowmobiles, after the first snowfall of the season, sound like the howl of coyotes. They move in packs, at night, also.

November 29, 1994

The Death of Flowers

Is there a connection between my "loose leg," which Hans is disturbed by and criticizes me often for in my riding lessons, and the "looseness" I feel between my conscious self and my subconscious? I don't feel "whole"; my important issues within my subconscious mind can't seem to find pathways to the surface. Yet I know that part of my mind is working so hard. Last night Hans said I was talking in my sleep most of the night, and I could feel a headache developing during the middle of the night also.

* I need more connectedness and intensity of experience, stronger connection with my legs when riding.

Is riding well a pathway to the un- (or sub) conscious? Step by step moving forward?

December 14, 1994

I have resolved to take care of my passions, like children, and not abort them. "What a beautiful choice." The violent thoughts as well as the desired, beautiful ones.

That anger I feel, what anger I'm giving life to! What will it, in turn, create? A hostile, troubled character? A poem which tears open a thought, a poem which rips open a chest and pulls out a heart? (Remember that dream of a surgeon sawing open a breast bone and lifting out a heart?)

Perhaps I have a need for much *rougher* prose or poetry than I had been anticipating. I've been wanting to write something jewel-like, but maybe what I *want* isn't exactly the point.

The hatchet sank into my knee. My hands were numb from the vibrations of peeling the bark from oak fence posts all day long. First I crouched from the pain, then when I stood up I was so dizzy. It was a beautiful evening in summer. A weightless sky. A light yellow, indistinct sun, a washed-out blue and my lover didn't want to stop what he was doing up on the hill in order to help. So I walked down the ridge road myself and found the simple stream, not much of a stream really. I sat in it in my blue jeans. I tore the leg off of one where I had sliced into my knee, and watched the blood make a delicate weave with the water. The water and sky the same empty color, like 7-Up.

"Everything that's there, belongs."

December 17, 1994

The Lessons of King Lear: Folly—Wisdom

Shamu did really well today. Riding him as a hunter. Perhaps it is not good for him to be constantly "dressaged."

Hans and I had several "discussions" today, and we each caused pain, I believe. Toward the end, Hans reminded me that he "nursed me" for several years, comforting me through years of screaming in my sleep. Somehow I was able to tell him that I still haven't regained trust, no matter how much I may want to. The deeper levels of my heart don't trust. I told him that if he had a better understanding of psychology that he might understand what I mean.

That lack of trust, having that, has been my secret. I never thought that I would tell that to Hans. I was hoping to spare him. I have no idea what he thinks.

I felt shot full of holes.

Line of poetry:

"I've been shot full of holes."

* Remember how I pushed Jay on several occasions?

I also told Hans how he's not an easy man. "You just aren't." He then said that I was not an easy woman.

(to be expanded on later. a.m. wearable art)

The snow is like a beaded mohair sweater.

Beaded pearl.

First the brown and white scarf in garden stitch. Mom keeps in the car for emergencies.

* The horse blanket I tried to knit as a little girl. White with apple-green hearts. Now in a tapestry, without the hunting scenes.

Valor, etc. * Women have valor. *

December 21, 1994

I have run out of time this evening but I thought I'd quickly get down a few notes. I took my last box of Iowa things to the Goodwill store today: a nice turntable and speakers, a cassette player and an old radio. I believe all of it is in good working order.

I feel that I have become transformed within the past week: I don't feel well when I don't write at least half an hour every day. That expression has suddenly become such an important part of my life. I am trying to do right by those inner workings and find a connection.

Remember some of those pizza suppers I had with Jay were in downtown Decorah? Was it at Godfather's Pizza? I wonder what we kept talking about. (I was going to write a book called "The Language of Horses.")

He must have suffered with a lot of pain.

Remember how, that time my parents came down to stay overnight in Decorah, I went back to the farm to stay with Jay: How incredibly dangerous that was. Was that the same night that he insisted we go to the Harlan's for a lengthy talk?

December 23, 1994

I didn't ride today. I needed a day of rest, up to a point. I still lunged????? a few horses, did two loads of laundry, moved the last of my things from the east apartment and did some reading—that's what I consider a sick day. We went through with the sale [of the farm] and it's one of the most painful things I've ever done. The feelings of grief will last a long time, I think. How can we have sold the farm?

But at the same time, I believe that this is the true beginning of our marriage. We've spoken about so many things this past week. I told Hans that I first fell in love with him in 9th grade, when I came up to buy a horse. A week ago, he reminded me how he nursed me "Back to Health," getting me through all those nightmares. We've had frank discussions about finances, and what it is going to be like for the next several years.

That image I had when I was ill this morning: Peoples' mouths, tense with anger, extreme anger——mouthy turns into a festering sore——lips, sexuality.

This is one of the first times that I've allowed an ugly image to happen. I've so much believed in the beautiful.

It seems, again, that I must write, now, every day. I become physically ill when I've skipped writing in the evening before. My deep thoughts and voices are insisting on their freedom. Kari, the horse, has "thoughts" also, and he supposedly is my "twin." How does this correlate with my situation? The static, the inability to express the tenseness, the oversensitivity to noise and distractions, and how all these things make him seemingly less trainable than other horses.

Remember Jan's thought about how she thinks jumping is more of a 50-50 proposition as opposed to dressage. Depending on the horse's judgment.

Challenge: How to allow for the horse's expressiveness.

December 24, 1994

From Jamestown this morning I heard the tortured cry "It's too late for me—save yourselves."

Christmas Day, 1994

The concept of "Inversions"

* an inverted horse

* Shakespeare's *King Lear*

* how in my poetry the choice of words could somehow exhibit the inversion

The fascination I have with car emblems. As I'm driving I focus in on them as cars drive by me in the other lanes. I feel a "kinship" with other Volkswagen drivers and owners. Remember the young man who stopped me on the streets in Stillwater and we discussed Volkswagens? He was really an expert, and he loved my new car.

Working Titles for My Own Story

* Horse Killer

* The Assassinated Horse

* An Assassination of Horses

* The Murdered Horses

Get a list of their names. Look at the folder on the bottom of Jay's briefcase.

The horses and myself were shot in the same way. However, the horses were not as fortunate as I. They lost their lives.

* A non-linear memoir, bits of the past, imagery welling up and affecting the present life of the troubled woman.

The Dangerous Saltwell colt named "Praise the Lord" and how that owner cruelly relayed information about the murdered horses.

The woman didn't realize that Jay had murdered the horses until she herself had been shot. The sheriff's revelations (They knew) (So much of the town knew, although she insisted to me that "He wouldn't touch a fly.") Also, remember in one of Marjorie's drunken episodes she told Jay that she became an alcoholic because "Jay was nuts." That's why. She didn't know how to cope with it. At the time, I thought she was merely being cruel, trying to hurt him. But there was truth in it. He was nuts. But I cared for him deeply.

Vague stories about the "mob" wanting to come after Jay and that's why the horses were killed.

* This group of horses seemed to live on in Jay's mind long after the death of them. He had them shipped to various places in Kentucky, Florida, Arkansas or California, and he still owned them. He had imaginary talks on the phone with trainers and often their children. Sometimes he would actually talk with a trainer on the phone, but it was probably about life and race track life in general. Or he would take imaginary flights on charter airplanes to visit his animals, dine with the trainer, etc.

Jay

Stroking the cats, his loving behavior with the cats and his care of them.

His mad language. His soft belly, exposed because the buttons on the lower part of his shirt were always unbuttoned.

How he tried to sabotage the trip to Minneapolis. With whiskey. He drove the truck through the mud, and mysteriously the left spring on that one side of the trailer was broken. We discovered it halfway up to Minneapolis.

The fire and the tractor. The fire department had to be called out to put out a big grass fire and he was so upset when I asked him to be more careful.

How at one point he asked me to kill him with a knife in my studio apartment.

Remember how jealous Hans became once when he realized that Jay had stayed overnight? And how Hans wouldn't listen to my explanation until later.

* Opening lines: description of the shadows on the snow at night, and then perhaps a description of Marjorie sitting on her throne, the fuchsia chair covered with a powder blue satin blanket. The rotting dead mice underneath. How she must have looked when she was younger. Crocheted gloves and big hats.

The first time I met her she was lying on the cement, drunk, and I believe she had broken a hip (one of the first times).

How she took a piss outside a major liquor store in La Crosse. She had only a light, see-through "chiffon" nightgown, cut to knee length (roughly), with a scissors.

* The stories of Bob, and the kind of man he was: how he said he and his friends burned a house down after several years of living in it.

A Lear. His dangerousness.

January 3, 1995

Leaving home—the concept of—Does the analogy of a ship leaving port work? Returning to port?

* Begin discussion about the shooting—material for writing my own story.

In the Decorah Hospital, remember how the nurse said, "He's a goner." And also, they had forgotten to pull the curtain between us, so I could look over at him.

* Before I was lifted into the ambulance, remember how worried I was about losing my—where did this come from—purse? Remember years earlier when my mother bought me a purse and told me to keep my treasures in there. (The small taupe evening bag).

* Perhaps one of the most shattering moments for me was in the Decorah Hospital when Dr. Bakken would not hold my hand, as I was begging him to do. It was bad enough to have to beg, but then to beg and not have him come through for me. I felt like such an outcast at that moment, like

I'd have to do this all on my own. The scarlet letter. Was he a coward? Or was there more to it than that? I believe it was at that moment that I lost all trust, all faith in other humans. (Tell this to Emilio in next letter, the issue of trust).

* Hands are so beautiful. Expressive, useful. One reason I want to write is because it employs my hands. Writing letters to me is a form of hand holding. To carry some of these thoughts further, have I been too heavy-handed at times with the horses because of not letting my hands speak (write) in these other ways?

Remember the *Age of Innocence* (the movie) and how beautifully the passions were expressed through the hands. I saw this movie with Jan!

January 4, 1995

I have been exhausted by my emotions today. Sorrow for the shooting itself and also a sense of longing for a certain kind of love. For the first time, in a way, I've let love touch me, really touch me, and it's a bit overwhelming. What can I do with it? What should I?

I have a history of being loved and not loved at the same time, by the same man. Or I've asked men to love me who aren't capable of it. To me it's a form of dissembling. *Making a pretense of loving the unlovable.* That's all I felt I could do, all the farther I felt I could go. *I've had myself convinced of my limitations, which may not really exist.* For as long as I can remember I've felt that love is something indirect, dissembling. But yesterday I felt the possibility of the directness of love. It's too new. I don't know what to make of it.

He seems to message the bruised part of my brain.

I'd like to write a poem about the office, the comfort of the office.

One of the reasons I wanted to hold Dr. Bakken's hand years ago (in 1986) was that if I did die, I wanted some control over my last vision. I wanted to gaze at an object of beauty. The human hand seemed all that was available, and all its expressiveness. He refused. He refused to comfort me. He refused to let me look at his hand.

I think it was Jay who latched onto me.

January 5, 1995

The piano. She dives into the (?), but resurfaces.

Use this imagery within the poem. Finding the beaded pearl at the bottom of the knitting bag. The array of dark yarns—describe.

What did (does) this experience mean to you?

A big thing in the hospital and afterward was that people kept telling me what experiences meant to *them*. They would relate stories about their family member who had committed suicide, etc. The sheriff and policemen were no different.

From a conversation between Carole and her longtime speech pathologist, Anne Gerber. Anne is co-author with Emilio DeGrazia of *Shamu, Solemn & Splash, The Creative Writing of Carole Jayne Stoa Senn* (Lost Lake Folk Art, 2017).

Anne: Let me read everything we have so far: "I had a repetitive dream with Shamu, Orval, Hans and me. Shamu and I were trotting and cantering in a dressage show at the fairgrounds. Hans was coaching me and Orval was sitting in the bleachers holding my horse blanket." I want to get some feeling into it. Do you remember your feelings in the ring?

Carole: I was peaceful riding.

Anne: Was it important to your peacefulness that Hans and Orval were there?

Carole: Uh-huh.

Anne: Do you want to add that? "I was peaceful riding knowing Orval and Hans were there with me."

Carole: Uh-huh. Uh-huh … and I was in heaven.

Anne: Were you physically in heaven, or the expression "I was in heaven?"

Carole: (To the choice that she was physically in heaven) Uh-huh.

Anne: So now we have: "I had a repetitive dream with Shamu, Orval, Hans and me. Shamu and I were trotting and cantering in a dressage show at the fairgrounds. Hans was coaching me and Orval was sitting in the bleachers holding my horse blanket. I was in Heaven."

Carole: Capital, capital, heaven.

Anne: Is that it?

Carole: And then, Amen.

Carole, her dream in her own words—

I would like to write three books:
My memoir, entitled *Shamu*,
and two horse novels,
Splash and *Solemn*.

Moral hazard in a haphazardly amoral era
Opinion by Tom Driscoll

Again I measure the rate of Fall by the wither and wilt and the wicked wick of green into brown out a second story window facing the bluff rising behind the house. Colorful leaves bed the small plateau where Beth and I have buried so many beloved animals, but the trees are not bare; they quickly rust. Again, the end is near. After a few silent words with Mel, Brother & Elsie, August & Pepper, Mr. Squeak & Miss Blue, I retreat on a warm, sunny October day to the security of my office to start writing again.

Only numbers leech out at first, statistics. My fingers twitch—mass homicide of 59 total strangers, the mass wounding of an additional 527 total strangers by a shooter bunkered 32 stories above his concert-going targets surrounded by 19 assault rifles and ammunition enough to rain down death for 10 to 15 hellish minutes, bringing the total number of mass shootings in the U.S. this year alone to 273 … oops, this just in: 274.

The vocabulary of public safety has been largely factored down into bystander statistics and rhetorical gun rights gas, shoot 'em up movies, video games and thumbnail grids, portraits of the killed and injured reduced to a media equivalent of a mass grave.

Numbed beyond shock, We the People grapple for proper words to express outrage.

I remember the first time I heard *Your student's safety is our first priority* by **Nicole Borg**, read by the poet a couple of years ago now on an inclement winter night at a café in Winona, Minnesota. Nicole is not an imposing woman—not in size—but strap a metaphoric sidearm on her and "disengage the safety" and suddenly her voice booms. The vocabulary used to describe this secondary school English teacher, a mom and a poet, clearing classrooms one-by-one until she finally confronts a school shooter provides much needed counter-imagery in this age of mass shootings: one every single day of the year.

> I instruct my students
> to no longer be still, quiet,
> but a moving, angry target

'I'll be shooting blanks,' or so the Teacher College-trained educator promises when the 'emergency drill' begins, and I can't help but for just a second to think of Wizard School, only Harry Potter's magic wand is a handgun. Then, after invoking first-person-shooter video games, the poet menaces all of us, claws bared in defense of her pint-sized charges—

> With steady hands
> I will lay that fucker out.

Coarse language indeed for a teacher of third-graders, but Nicole's is not a poem for children; it is a new lexicon intended for adults who are forever sickened by Sandy Hook and Columbine, and all the shot-up, traumatized schools in-between. It's a poetic threat, a vexed glove-slap to the puss of Second Amendment originalists, the NRA, and, to borrow from the old lexicon, Gun Nuts. Be forewarned. History keeps happening, and Who are terrorized by Guns in America may turn on the Who believe gun-ownership symbolizes freedom than mass murder tramples on freedom.

> the students will toss their pint-sized
> Stetsons into the air
> and with their Tony Llamas boots,
> stomp on his still warm dead body

When you look at the contents of this issue through the lens of public peril due to the actions of others, strangers often, you can parse a wonderful, if at times dark, commentary on society and culture in our lifetimes. Two contributors in particular take that lens and look in a completely different direction from Nicole. If Nicole's guardian-shooter is a Defender, then **C.J. Pickens** is a Perpetrator, **Carole Stoa Senn** is a Target; and by the way, the rest of us, we're not so innocent Bystanders.

Right into the dark is where *Sin and X* takes the reader, a dark wild side of short fiction adapted from **C.J. Pickens'** unpublished novel *SIN*. I don't quite know how to tag this piece except to call it fantasy guns-love-money fiction, guns being the currency, love being mostly physical—a

dependency as powerful as any drug—and money being the only drug powerful enough to shield the protagonist, a teenage girl named Ebony 'EB' Ivory, 'Sin' for short, from the lonely cycle of foster homes, group homes, street crime and jail. (Names are important in Pickens' story. Everyone has lots of them.)

When Sin's mother's live-in boyfriend, Zayne 'Blu' Walker, and the only father Sin ever knew is murdered in Kansas City, she visits the Walker kin. To her surprise, she receives much needed familial comfort, and in lieu of love, respect—oh, and a $160,000 inheritance. What does Sin do? She considers her options, which is the plot in a nutshell. The storytelling structure is skillful for a first-time writer, not a dance really, not through the carnage Sin and X (aka Bubbles) wreak on their enemies, but an introspective futuristic leap between the present and the past.

The story starts as future option one is acted out in the near past. Sin and X murder a drug kingpin who betrayed them. Remember, the speaker uttering this rough prose is not even twenty years old.

> Both hollow points ripped through his chest, suffocating what little life he had left, a dozen still eyes wide and glossy, staring into that inevitable eternity. The Head Honcho, King of Scandalous Kansas, gelded in under sixty seconds. Yep, just that easy.

In another time—the arc of a teenager's narrative spanning weeks that feel like years—Sin expresses what it is she really seeks, what guns (murder), love (lesbian) and money (lots of it) and nothing else, can achieve for her.

> The sun was peeking over the horizon. The morning air cool even for June in the Midwest. The joyous chirping from a flock of birds that flew above stopped me in my tracks for a second. In that moment, those birds represented my commitment to denouncing the game. I was going to

be free, free as them birds chirping overhead.

This is pathological writing, a deep exploration of a violent fantasy drawn from an impulsive collage of personal experiences that beg explanation. C.J Pickens is a pastiche of legal names for Cassandra S., the author. I've been receiving typewritten correspondence from the Women's Correctional Facility in Vandalia, Missouri, for much of the past year. Cassandra has served seven years of a mandatory twenty-year sentence for manslaughter and "armed criminal action."

> I always knew that I wanted to be a writer and knew that I had a story to tell, however, it wouldn't be until I was thirty years old, incarcerated and facing a life sentence that I'd find the stability and develop the discipline to follow my passion.

The bizarre saga of gun violence in America comes to a full stop when Cassandra straps a pen on her hip instead of a sidearm and begins to write.

> One day, while doing another extended stay in solitary confinement, I asked myself, "How can I change my life right now, with what I have available?" Well, if you don't know, all one gets in isolation are clothes and stationaries. So, I picked up my ink pen and began writing my biography. Sixty-three days later I finished the first draft. Dubious as to if my story were to ever be published, and

> would I want to be perceived in such a manner by the public, I decided against it. In doing so, the fictitious character named Ebony Ivory was born. Sin. She became who I now call "my alter ego," and the means to tell my story.

That brings We the hand-wringing Bystanders to the Targets. Knowing that victimhood in America is fraught with misinterpretation to the point of being pejorative, Target seems strangely less of a pejorative. Certainly, targeted victimhood as a stereotype of weakness is explored, laid bare and transcended in *Shamu, Splash & Solemn: The Creative Writing of Carole Jayne Stoa Senn*, co-authored by Anne Gerber and Emilio DeGrazia (Lost Lake Folk Art, 2017).

Carole Stoa Senn is a poet and essayist who writes (like Cassandra in many ways) from the mandatory security of a solitary mind, a circumstance forced upon her by gross domestic violence—gun violence, and when six shots failed to kill her, running her over with a pickup truck—and a devastating brain aneurysm that left her wheelchair bound and unable to communicate without assistance.

Anne Gerber is Carole's speech pathologist and facilitated the more recent poems. Emilio DeGrazia has taught English to hundreds of undergraduate students, young writers, including Carole. With Emilio's help, Carole produced letters, journal entries and poems in the 1990s during the healing period between being shot and run over by her husband (who then took his own life) and her crippling brain aneurysm.

> Perhaps I have a need for much *rougher* prose or poetry than I had been anticipating. I've been wanting to write something jewel-like, but maybe what I *want* isn't exactly the point.

Exactly what is the point is for Carole? It is best described as complex and closely held.

That lack of trust, having that, has been my secret. I never thought that I would tell that to Hans. I was hoping to spare him. I have no idea what he thinks. I felt shot full of holes.

Back to gun violence. Back to public safety, the right of every Bystander to not only feel safe, but to experience safety as a basic freedom. Carole's former husband killed himself with a single shot. It's tempting to assign swift justice; but by-far the greatest number of American gun victims are males who commit suicide. In the case of domestic assault using guns, a Federally mandated waiting period is analogous to a cooling off period, a timeout between whatever urge drives homicide, and buying a gun. Waiting periods would not have spared Carole. Her husband was a farmer. He raised horses, Carole's passion. She suspected he suffered from mental disease. Better rural mental health services and tighter mental health screening of gun purchases might have helped. Then again, maybe not.

He fumbled in the case and pulled out a gun. My first reaction was not fear, just wonderment at what he was doing. I quickly learned that the gun was for me as he pointed it my way. I said, "No! No! No!" Despite my pleas, he began shooting. First at my heart, followed by my left forearm and left elbow, with the final shot to the back of my head at my neck and the base of my spine. Seven or eight bullets entered me with a warm sensation. I then had a vision during the shooting that I was in Heaven and saw the Son, Father and Holy Ghost in bodily form. Heaven then quickly vanished and the reality of the situation lay before me. I escaped from the stopped truck. I began running, running in the cornfields to the highway.

Through all the adversity life imposed on Carole, she has continued to think and to write. With an indomitable will to see the glass half full, Carole continues to create outstanding works of art.

Carole: I was peaceful riding.

Anne: Was it important to your peacefulness that Hans and Orval were there?

Carole: Uh-huh.

Anne: Do you want to add that? "I was peaceful riding knowing Orval and Hans were there with me."

Carole: Uh-huh. Uh-huh … and I was in heaven.

Anne: Were you physically in heaven, or the expression "I was in heaven?"

Carole: (To the choice that she was physically in heaven) Uh-huh.

Anne: So now we have: "I had a repetitive dream with Shamu, Orval, Hans and me. Shamu and I were trotting and cantering in a dressage show at the fairgrounds. Hans was coaching me and Orval was sitting in the bleachers holding my horse blanket. I was in Heaven."

Carole: Capital, capital, heaven.

Anne: Is that it?

Carole: And then, Amen.

The clocks never stop tocking off seasons. Forgive the tautology, but Time is the great Moral Hazard of all Time. After all, we buy time like government subsidized insurance believing like damn fools in time's mysterious corrective and healing power. Then we wait, sometimes for an eternity, to see if we've made a smart purchase. America simply cannot buy more time on the gun rights issue. The Second Amendment in all its voluble brevity was written for another time. It is not a guarantee for eternal gun rights. Over time, We the People have come to better understand that the insurance baked into the Second Amendment has to be balanced against the security of the many guarantors of "a well-regulated militia." We're all guarantors of the Constitution and the Bill of Rights: Defenders, Perpetrators, Targets and Bystanders: we safeguard freedom as sure as any deadeye gun owner.

For too long the righteous argument that more guns in the hands of America's self-proclaimed protectors of freedom makes us safer has gotten the last whack-in beating the dead horse. Whack whack. Ready access to powerful guns and deadly ammunition makes us all less safe. Federal, state and local law enforcement are armed to the teeth. Ask gun owners, Is law enforcement the enemy? Lawlessness masquerading as lawful is the real enemy, my friends.

No more ink will I waste beating the dead horse. As an editor, I think the Second Amendment needs amending. In any event, I submit to you the extremely diverse voices of three very articulate writers.

Poetry, essays and literary fiction—like contributions made by all the tremendous writers featured in this issue—provide many levels of quiet and question, contemplation and pleasure. It's called reading. When the pen is loaded, *the pen is mightier than the sword*. Now it's time to disengage the safety, readers & writers, and let's lay that fucker out.

The 2nd Amendment

A well regulated militia, being necessary to the security of a free state, the right of the people to keep and bear arms, shall not be infringed.

Look for these new releases from SHIPWRECKT BOOKS at your local bookseller and online
at www.shipwrecktbooks.com.

www.ingramcontent.com/pod-product-compliance
Lightning Source LLC
Chambersburg PA
CBHW082050220626

47052CB00006B/1202